This enchanting new book is also an important new book, inviting readers to reflect on an often neglected part of the spiritual life: friendship. Using examples from the scriptures, from the lives of the saints, and from her own life, Mary DeTurris Poust shows us how love is connected to friendship, how charity is connected to companionship, and how loving relationships with one another lead to friendship with God. Helpful, wise, provocative, sensible, and always inspirational, this is a book for all Christian disciples, whom Jesus called "friends."

James Martin, S.J.
Author of *The Jesuit Guide to (Almost) Everything*

In today's world, the word "friend" has taken on an entirely new context. With her marvelous book *Walking Together*, author Mary DeTurris Poust reminds us of the joys and blessings of true spiritual friendship. By sharing faith-filled examples from scriptures, saintly role models, and her own life, Mary paves the way for us to encounter and treasure true spiritual companions in our own lives. Thoughtful reflection questions and meditations at the end of each chapter make this the perfect resource for group study or personal spiritual development.

Lisa M. Hendey
Author of *The Handbook for Catholic Moms*

This exquisite book will help others open their eyes to the beauty and meaning that luminously exist within their friendships.

Donna-Marie Cooper O'Boyle
Host of EWTN's *Everyday Blessings for Catholic Moms*

WALKING TOGETHER

DISCOVERING *the* CATHOLIC TRADITION *of* SPIRITUAL FRIENDSHIP

MARY DeTURRIS POUST

ave maria press A m P notre dame, indiana

Founded in 1865, Ave Maria Press is a ministry of the Indiana
Province of Holy Cross.

www.avemariapress.com

ISBN-10 1-59471-209-3   ISBN-13 978-1-59471-209-8

Cover image © superstock.com.

Cover and text design by Andy Wagoner.

Printed and bound in the United States of America.

Library of Congress Cataloging-in-Publication Data

Poust, Mary DeTurris.
    Walking together : discovering the Catholic tradition of spiri-
tual friendship / Mary DeTurris Poust.
        p. cm.
    Includes bibliographical references.
    ISBN-13: 978-1-59471-209-8 (pbk.)
    ISBN-10: 1-59471-209-3 (pbk.)
    1. Friendship--Religious aspects--Christianity. 2. Friendship-
-Religious aspects--Catholic Church. I. Title.
    BV4647.F7P68 2010
    241'.6762088282--dc22
                                                    2010008577

For
Bill, Dorothy, and Ken,
who have blessed my life
with their love, wisdom,
faith, and friendship;

and for
Rob,
who was called home far too soon
but left a lasting imprint on my heart.

Contents

Foreword

Mary DeTurris Poust believes that spiritual friends are not only lovely to hold close to one's heart, but are also incredibly vital as we journey toward heaven. She points out that Jesus sent the disciples out "never alone, always in pairs" because he knew they would need that close companionship. Throughout her book, brilliantly and ever so tenderly, Mary unwraps every layer of the bonds of friendship to reveal each unique facet, giving us much to ponder. Through a wealth of anecdotes, personal stories, and wisdom from saints and others, she enlightens us to the reality that we are all "hungry for a real connection" and for "deeper, lasting friendships in this world where so much is temporary."

I am very grateful that God has arranged a spiritual and sisterly friendship between Mary and me. We both share a love for our Catholic faith, and we are each thoroughly familiar with the details—great and small—that matter most inside our domestic churches. And to top it off, we are both Catholic authors who downright love to weave words together, hoping and praying to inspire others.

Many times one just knows when an encounter with another is meant to last much longer than for only those short initial moments. Mary contacted me several years ago because she was given my name to interview for an article she was writing. I sensed while we spoke that the two of us could easily become friends. If we lived near one another, I was sure that we would want to take walks together out in nature, savor a cup of tea, or sip at a glass of wine if we were blessed with the time to share one another's company. I had no doubt that we would naturally converse all the while about family life, any aspect of our faith journeys, or our writing endeavors. We would be spiritual, sisterly friends!

In God's providence, Mary and I did indeed get back in touch later on and forged a friendship through the years as we compared notes about our writing lives and spiritual lives as well. Mary is a keeper, no doubt about it. She's one of those exceptional friends that you know would move her freshly made pot of healthy soup off the burner for a bit if I happened to call her in dire need at dinner time.

Her life echoes that beautiful sentiment in Sirach: "A faithful friend is a sturdy shelter" (6:14). So, it's truly no surprise to me that Mary put pen to paper and fingers to keys to share honestly and deeply of her own life to write this exquisite book. I know it will help others open their eyes to the beauty and meaning that luminously exists within their friendships while also assisting them to discover the friendships "that are hidden in plain sight." She brings a new awareness of the necessity to tend and nourish each one.

In a world where technology supposedly connects us, "we really couldn't be more disconnected from those special spiritual friendships that could bring warm companionship and support." *Walking Together* encourages us to focus on the essentials and prods us on to both gather and impart love through all of our friendships, for each one is "an endless loop of mutual care and concern."

Mary conveys that "no matter how we choose to bond—in prayer, over coffee, through honest conversations, with humor or music, in the midst of a service project—spiritual friendships will grow and deepen. And most of us will be changed from the inside out." I am convinced that when you have read this book, you will be genuinely enriched in your own friendships and changed for the better "from the inside out," and you will have found a dear spiritual friend and sister in Mary DeTurris Poust.

Enjoy your journey. May you be richly blessed by God's grace!

Donna-Marie Cooper O'Boyle

Host of EWTN's *Everyday Blessings for Catholic Moms*

Acknowledgments

As with each of the books I have written, my acknowledgments can begin with only one person: my husband, Dennis, who never fails to get behind my writing efforts with enthusiasm and encouragement and who serves as my editor on the home front, reading every word and offering valuable insights and suggestions. While I always value his professional expertise, I am even more grateful for his unconditional love, his confidence in me, and his sense of humor. He is my best friend—spiritual and otherwise—and I am blessed to have him in my life.

A big hug and lots of love go out to our three children— Noah, Olivia, and Chiara. Every time I set out to write a book, they know it will mean less time for them and more quiet for me, two things that aren't always easy to maneuver in a busy household. And yet they always come through for me, not only with their willingness to put things on hold while I work but with their unbridled excitement over the very fact that I am writing a book.

I would also like to thank Cathy Odell for her work on this book and everyone at Ave Maria Press, including Robert Hamma, Susana Kelly, Maria Boyer, and Amanda Williams.

Since this is a book about friendship, it's probably pretty obvious that I need to thank some of my friends. I have to start with Msgr. William Benwell, a spiritual friend *par excellence*. I am so grateful for his friendship, his love, and his never-ending encouragement. I also need to thank Dorothy

Armstrong and Ken Giovanelli, who may not realize the lasting impact their friendship has had on me. Although we rarely get to see each other anymore, their openness about their own spiritual journeys and their willingness to share their wisdom and their love has been a true blessing in my life. To all those friends who have helped me on my path through their examples of faith and their witness to the Gospel, thank you. And where would I be without the friends who keep my spirits up amid the chaos of everyday life? Abby, Michelle D., Robyn, Michele B., and all my Cornerstone sisters—I am so grateful for your presence in my life.

As I mention in this book, friendship is first formed among family members, and my family is no exception. My mother, Irene DeTurris, truly was my best friend, and she continues to shape my life even twenty-two years after her death, but it would be an incomplete picture to stop there. My father, Salvatore DeTurris; my sister, Tricia; and my brother, Fred; all have played a critical role in making me who I am today, and I thank them for the love they continue to share with me. To the rest of my family: my grandmother, Helen DeTurris; my stepmother, Doreen; and all of my aunts, uncles, and cousins—especially my aunts Margaret Robertson and Louise Mangan, who are like second mothers to me—thank you for being in my life and for being who you are. I love you all.

Introduction

Spiritual friendship. Those two simple words have changed my life, and I'm hoping that they will soon change yours. Long before this book was even a glimmer in my mind's eye, those words took up residence deep within my heart and soul and began to reshape the way I think about the key people who have influenced—and continue to influence—my life in powerful ways. It was as if my eyes were opened to a whole other dimension of spirituality, a world that was right there in front of me, waiting to be savored.

The culture we live in isn't always encouraging when it comes to making and sustaining lasting friendships. We need friendships that go beyond pleasantries exchanged at the end of the driveway, or waves from our car as we head to the grocery store. We may be more connected than ever before, thanks to e-mail and the Internet and cell phones. And yet, we have never been so disconnected from the people who could add warmth and support and companionship to our increasingly isolated lives. Spiritual friendship can play a critical role in reconnecting us to those people who share our beliefs, our values, our ideals, our goals.

My journey into the heart of spiritual friendship did not start with a conscious search for connection in my life. I have a loving family and wonderful friends. So, I wasn't feeling particularly adrift in that department. My journey began by accident, when I bumped into St. Francis de Sales and fell in love with the writings of this seventeenth-century bishop

whose ideas and spiritual advice hold up surprisingly well
to my twenty-first-century sensibilities. Up until that point,
I had known St. Francis primarily as the patron saint of
writers, since that is my life's work. When I discovered his
writings, it was as though someone had opened up the book
of my heart and started reading. I read his letters, I bought
his books, and I began searching for everything I could find
about this beloved saint and the deep spiritual friendship
he shared with St. Jane de Chantal.

Then, in the midst of what some might call an obses-
sion, I went to Good Friday Stations of the Cross. As the
Sixth Station approached, I looked down at the program
to join the rest of the congregation in reading our part: "A
faithful friend is a sturdy shelter. He who finds one finds a
treasure. . . ." The words from Sirach were like a thunder-
bolt. It was confirmation of what I had guessed all along.
This quest to understand spiritual friendship was not
something I could ignore anymore. I needed to dive in and
figure out where it was meant to lead me.

And that brings us to where we are today. Several years
have passed since that Good Friday, but my excitement
over the concept of spiritual friendship has not dimmed.
In fact, it is stronger than ever. When I started this book, I
was aware of a few deep spiritual friends who had blessed
my life with their examples of faith and their willingness to
help me along that same path. By the end of this book, I began to take notice of the "minor" players in my friendship
story, the people who tend to stay on the periphery of my
life but who still manage to have an impact through their

words, their actions, even their silent but constant witness to the Gospel.

My hope is that this book will do for you what it has done for me—open your eyes to the gift of friendship that is right there in front of you. I hope that by sharing stories of friendship and by tracing the examples of spiritual friendship throughout our faith history, you will be able to recognize the spiritual companions who are walking beside you on your own journey toward God.

You can pick up this book and read any chapter that sounds interesting to you at the moment. Or, you can start at the beginning and read it all the way through. The earlier chapters will provide you with a broad overview of spiritual friendship. The later chapters get progressively more practical, providing concrete suggestions for finding and nurturing spiritual friendships in your own life.

Each chapter is punctuated by a personal story as well as stories from other people who have been willing to allow us to peer into the most intimate and deep friendships in their lives. In addition, every chapter takes examples from the lives of saints and saints-to-be—some whom you may recognize with no introduction, like Francis and Clare of Assisi, to others whose stories may be new to you, like Jordan of Saxony and Diana d'Andalo. Step into their lives and watch how they allowed their faith in God to transform their friendships into true spiritual partnerships.

At the end of each chapter, you will find discussion questions. I hope you'll take some time to read them, think about them, pray about them, journal about them, talk about them in a group—whatever feels most comfortable and helpful to you. Then take a few minutes to pause and meditate on the spiritual reflection at the end of each chapter.

Whether you are reading this book on your own or with a group, you will be surrounded by friends at the turn of every page—the friends from your own life who come to mind as you read about the gift of spiritual companionship, and the friends from history who remind us that this path toward God is never a solitary journey but one of community, friendship, and love.

At my children's preschool, they say a prayer of peace and friendship that originated with Mahatma Gandhi. That prayer seems like an especially appropriate way to end this introduction and begin our journey into the heart of spiritual friendship:

> I offer you peace. I offer you love.
> I offer you friendship. I see your beauty.
> I hear your cry. I feel your pain.
> My wisdom flows from a higher Source.
> I salute that Source in you.
> Let us work together.

Chapter 1

Companionship:
A Friend for the Journey

A faithful friend is a sturdy shelter;
he who finds one finds a treasure.
A faithful friend is beyond price,
no sum can balance his worth.
A faithful friend is a life-saving remedy,
such as he who fears God finds;
For he who fears God behaves accordingly,
and his friend will be like himself.

—Sirach 6:14–17

We live in a world of contradictions, at least where friendship and social interaction are concerned. On the one hand, this is the age of the "global village," where we are connected to our employers, our families, our friends, and even our passing acquaintances by cell phones, faxes, e-mail, and wireless gadgets that allow us to communicate in the blink of an eye. On the other hand, we live in increasing isolation. The very technology that is supposed to make our lives so much easier and so much more integrated is, in actuality, cutting us off from face-to-face contact, leaving us with mostly virtual relationships that may supply superficial satisfaction but never feed our deeper need for something that touches the heart and soul.

1

In some ways, it would seem impossible to be isolated in this modern-day world. Even on vacation, we are usually plugged into a mind-numbing array of people, places, and social networking websites that allow us to occupy every free second in our harried lives. The problem is that despite all our "favorites" and "buddies" out there in the land of plenty, we are hungry for a real connection.

This need, this hunger, is nothing new. The desire for companionship and friendship dates back to the beginning of humanity. The Lord himself said: "It is not good for man to be alone" (Gn 2:18). Human beings are meant to have partners to journey with them through different phases of life. Whether we are married or single, we need solid friend-ships in our lives, relationships that go deeper than meeting for coffee once a week or catching a movie after work. While those kinds of friends are important, to be sure, most of us need someone—or several "someones"—who are not just friends, but spiritual friends.

Spiritual friends are those soul mates who share our spiritual longings and help us to become our own best selves. These special friendships are like life preservers that keep our heads above the murky waters of isolation and superficiality. Sure, it may be fun, even necessary, to have friends we can call to go out for cocktails or shopping, but it is even more important to have friends we connect with in a significant and lasting way.

But spiritual friendships are not always easy to recog-nize immediately. They may develop slowly over months or even years. They may burn brightly for several years and then fade a bit as we move into a different stage of our lives.

We may look back at an earlier time in our own lives and realize that what got us through a rough spot was an extraordinary friendship that seemed ordinary at the time.

Recognizing Those "Aha!" Moments

I remember when I landed my first job after college in the communications office of the Roman Catholic Diocese of Metuchen, New Jersey. I was commuting to a new town more than an hour's drive from my home in suburban New York. I was young and somewhat intimidated by my new responsibilities, which included everything from reporting for the weekly newspaper to writing scripts for a cable show to editing a monthly newsletter. And then I met Dorothy, the diocesan director of evangelization, whose office was just one floor above mine.

Upon first meeting, Dorothy's unbridled joy seemed almost too good to be true. Could someone really be this happy, I wondered. Her obvious love of God—and trust in his plan—was like something I had never witnessed before and, to be honest, haven't seen since. Whether it was something "minor," like an office argument, or something major, like the loss of her apartment, Dorothy's trust that God was in control never wavered.

I would often retreat to Dorothy's office for a dose of her calm and steady words of encouragement. Her generosity and kindness spilled over into personal time as well. She invited me to stay at her apartment any time I was working late or out on a date. I could come and go—whether Dorothy was there or not—as if her home was my home. I have many fond memories of sitting at Dorothy's little dining table with her, sharing a simple meal and talking for hours.

I'll never forget the first time I stayed at her house and was awakened around 5 a.m. to the sound of Dorothy singing "Morning Has Broken" before taking her dog Raphael out for a walk. I thought I had fallen through the rabbit hole and into an animated Disney feature. Surely the dog would be sweeping up the kitchen while birds cleaned the dishes. But Dorothy was—and still is—100 percent genuine, as is our friendship. It didn't matter that I was in my early twenties and Dorothy was nearing fifty when we first met. Our unlikely friendship was held together by something deeper than the typical ties of age or hobbies. We were bound by our shared faith and our desire to further that faith not only through prayer and service but also through friendship.

Dorothy soon became a spiritual mentor whose sunny disposition and solid faith began to influence my own actions and attitudes in dramatic ways. Through her peaceful acceptance of even difficult situations in her life, I began to see a new way of dealing with things.

It took a minor car accident to make me see just how much Dorothy's influence had changed me. I was driving my little Chevy Chevette up the Garden State Parkway during rush hour on my way home from my Metuchen job one night when I rear-ended the very large car in front of me. Something distracted me, maybe a song on the radio, maybe another car on the bumper-to-bumper drive, and I simply didn't stop in time. The driver of the car I hit flew into a panic, saying he was worried about his heart. Since his car didn't have so much as a scratch, he took off. He left me standing there alone in my high-heeled boots and black winter cape, wondering how I was going to move my unmovable car across three lanes of traffic. With the help of some good Samaritans, my car was pushed onto the shoulder, where I waited for the police and a tow truck. An hour or so later, I called my parents in incredibly good humor and told them with a bit of a chuckle that I was standing in a repair shop in Newark holding the grille of my car in my hands. I'm sure my composure must have unsettled them. In some ways, it unsettled me. No tears, no cursing, no shouts of "Why me?"

Dorothy's trust and peace were starting to rub off on me. Her friendship and real-life witness to the Gospel was beginning to influence my choices and my actions in profound and positive ways. With Dorothy's lessons of faith echoing in my head, I knew that I could choose to respond to my crisis of the moment with trust rather than fear or frustration. My car may have been in pieces, but because of what I was learning from this person who was put in my path at just the right time, my spirit was intact.

It was only much later that I realized that Dorothy is one of those rare spiritual friends who come into our lives when we least expect them but most need them. They walk with us—like the two disciples traveling together on the road to Emmaus—talking with us, teaching us, praying with us, bringing us closer each day to God and, in doing so, helping us reach our fullest and truest potential.

I am now close to the age Dorothy was when I first met her, and she is almost seventy-five. Although we rarely see each other anymore, Dorothy remains a spiritual role model for me. She is someone who can give my prayer life a jolt with just one short conversation. We are in the midst of planning a weekend visit, something that will be akin to a retreat from my perspective because to be in Dorothy's company is to be in the presence of true holiness.

When I called her recently, she had just finished praying the Rosary on her porch. I took the opportunity to tell her again about that car accident from long ago and how she influenced me without even knowing it. In true Dorothy fashion, she began talking about the power of Scripture and the prophets in her own life and how all God ever wanted of his people was for them to trust in Him.

"I don't need to know the future. God will meet me wherever I go," Dorothy said, sounding very much like the woman I first met twenty-five years ago. When I spoke about the importance of our friendship in my life, she summed up spiritual friendship perfectly: "We can draw on each other's strength because we can't be up all the time, because we care about one another. We are united in Christ, united through the Spirit. That's what you don't have in other friendships that are not spiritual friendships. There's a very strong bond there that you might not have with someone you just meet for cocktails."

Spiritual Friendship: A Definition

Our fiercely independent society tells us we can make it on our own. We don't need anything but a desire to succeed and a willingness to work hard. Well, that may be true in the business of the world, but it is certainly not true in the business of the spirit. We all need companions. Even happily

married people need friend companions because no one
person can fill every need, every spiritual longing, at every
moment of our lives.

As we change and grow—and all of us do—we are often
met on our path by people like us who can take our figurative hand and accompany us to the next stage in our journey,
the way Dorothy did for me all those years ago. Such companionship, when it is good and true, can strengthen not
only our relationship with God but with important people
in our lives—spouse, children, parents, friends. Spiritual
friendships feed our souls, and when our souls are nourished and calm and strong, we tend to handle the rest of our
lives with less friction and chaos.

A spiritual friend can offer insights and prayers, comfort
and encouragement when we are struggling with our children or a problem at work. We can pray with one another
—or for one another. We can talk about spiritual questions
that not everyone else wants to discuss. Whether we live
across the street or across the country, we can join our hearts
and minds and provide each other with a spiritual refuge.
Such companionship can bring us a deep sense of peace
that comes from knowing we are loved in a particular way,
that we are not alone, and that what we are longing for and
striving for is not so impossible or crazy after all. And all of
that, in turn, allows us to approach the rest of our relationships and responsibilities with a spirit of hope and a sense
of solidarity. It is powerful stuff.

The longing for spiritual friends is not some inven-
tion of contemporary pop psychology. Throughout history,
people have been drawn together by their love of God and

their desire to become more spiritually centered. This desire and need is something that crosses the boundaries of religious beliefs. Whether you are Jewish or Christian or Muslim, Buddhist or Hindu or Native American, you are likely to have a hunger for companionships and friendships that incorporate your deepest beliefs in a life-changing way. The Buddhists call it *kalyana mittata*. The ancient Celts call it *anam cara*. Spiritual friendship may have different names in different religions and cultures, but it comes down to the same principle: two people bound together by a love of God. It is even possible for two deeply spiritual people of different faiths to come together in a spiritual friendship that does not negate either's religion, but instead feeds and fosters the friends' individual beliefs.

Thomas Merton, the famed Trappist monk whose extensive writings on prayer, peace, and his own journey to Christianity have influenced countless people of all faiths, was good friends with the late Daisetz T. Suzuki, a famous Zen master. The two met and corresponded. In fact, in his book *Zen and the Birds of Appetite*, Merton wrote extensively about Suzuki, saying that meeting him was "like arriving at one's own home." His conversations with Suzuki were "unforgettable" and "extraordinary," he wrote.[1]

Of Thich Nhat Hanh, another Buddhist monk, Merton once wrote: "Thich Nhat Hanh is more my brother than many who are nearer to me in race and nationality, because he and I see things in exactly the same way."[2] Rather than present a stumbling block, their different beliefs became building blocks. The friends took elements of each other's spiritual traditions and used them to strengthen their own faith practices.

Spiritual friendship can spring up in unlikely places and between unlikely people. God works in mysterious but wonderful ways. The key element in any spiritual friendship, however, is the longing for a deeper relationship with our Creator, something that is evident from earliest recorded history.

Look back at the quote from the Book of Sirach that opened this chapter. In reading the passage again, it becomes obvious that deep friendship has long been valued as something beneficial, powerful, and even life giving. In the full verse (6:5–17), Sirach says that we may have a multitude of acquaintances but will find that our true friends number only "one in a thousand."

Sounding surprisingly in touch with our modern sensibilities, the verse reminds us that many people will choose to be our friends for the wrong reasons and will turn their backs on us when we are in need or are no longer useful. I believe our mothers referred to those sorts of people as "fairweather friends." A true friend, on the other hand, is like another self, someone who will stand beside you no matter how many slings and arrows are buzzing past your head; someone who is, as stated in the Book of Proverbs, eternally yours: *"He who is a friend is always a friend"* (Prv 17:17).

Aelred of Rievaulx, a twelfth-century Cistercian monk, wrote the book of *Spiritual Friendship*—literally. In his best-selling treatise on the depth and significance of God-centered friendship, Aelred brings a spiritual dimension to the ideas originally expressed in *De Amicitia* (*On Friendship*)

more than one thousand years earlier by Cicero, the Roman
orator, philosopher, and statesman.

Rievaulx called the true friend a "guardian of love" and
a "guardian of the spirit," and said that true friendship is a
"virtue by which spirits are bound by ties of love and sweet-
ness." He refers back to Cicero's De Amicitia, saying, "Even
the philosophers of this world have ranked friendship not
with things casual or transitory but with virtues which are
eternal."[3] In other words, true friendship lasts forever and
is inescapably bound by a deep love, not a romantic love
but a soul-level love that allows the friendship to withstand
things that might destroy a lesser friendship—disagreements, separation by time or distance, pressures from the
outside world.

Aelred breaks friendship down into three basic types:
carnal, which is based on vice and is indiscriminate; worldly, which is based on gain and a desire for possessions; and
spiritual, which is based on morals and "pursuits among
the just."[4] Spiritual or "true" friendship, he explains, constantly perfects itself, grounds itself in a similarity of lives
and morals, and incorporates benevolence and charity.[5]

What Does That Mean for Us Today?

At this point it should be clear that spiritual friendship, with
its focus on benevolence and justice and charity, is a far cry
from a simple night out with the girls. Spiritual friendship
is connected to our God-given mission, our calling to live
out our faith in the everyday world. That's because spiritual
friendships run deep. They bend with pressure but don't

break. They give with no prospect of taking. They are not about possession but about transformation.

Perhaps you can think of a friend or two who fit into that category. These are the friends with whom you can be completely yourself, the friends who may disagree with you from time to time but never consider walking away. They are the friends who bring you dinner when you're sick, pray for you when you're struggling, and remind you that you are never alone.

The good news is that spiritual friendship is available to every person—man or woman, Christian or non-Christian, young or old. But sometimes we need concrete models to guide us on our way. Fortunately, we can look to the saints, even to Jesus himself, for models of spiritual friendship at work. Throughout this book, famous saints and sages will serve as guides, offering real-life examples of what it means to be a spiritual friend. Through their letters, their prayers, their work, it will become clear that their spiritual friendships led them forward and closer to God on an almost daily basis. And spiritual friendships can do the same for each one of us.

Taking Stock of Your Life

Jesus had many followers and friends. There were a few who clearly had a special role in his life, and there were those who followed him from a distance, perhaps out of curiosity. When it came down to it, however, there was a very small group of people who stood out as his closest friends, his "spiritual" friends. Think back to the gospels. There was Martha and Mary and their brother, Lazarus, whose death

so devastated Jesus that he wept before raising him from
the dead. There was the "beloved" disciple, to whom Jesus bestowed the care of his own mother at the crucifixion.
There was Mary Magdalene, the disciple to whom Jesus first
appeared after his resurrection. And then, in a class by himself, there was Peter, absent from the foot of the cross but
living proof that true friendship can withstand the tough-
est trials—even rejection and self-centered fear. These were
no ordinary friends, but friends of the highest order. In a
terrifying time, when their own lives were at risk because
of their friendship with and belief in Jesus, they remained
true, even when they remained at a distance.

So how do we develop those kinds of friendships in this
kind of world? Jesus' relationships with his dearest friends
seem unattainable in our society. Jesus spent several years
with his spiritual friends, sharing intense experiences. His
spiritual friends gave up everything to follow him, even
when they weren't completely sure what Jesus' mission was
all about. Their lives were intertwined around each other
and, more importantly, around God. For us, these examples
serve not as an exact blueprint but as a broad model of the
kinds of relationships that are possible.

Jesus knew the importance of spiritual friendship. Think
about the way he sent out the disciples—never alone, always in pairs (Lk 10:1). And, in Matthew 18:20, Jesus says
that wherever "two or three are gathered together in my
name, there am I in the midst of them." Jesus knew that his
followers would need companionship. Just like those first
disciples, we are clearly not meant to walk this spiritual

journey alone. Spiritual friends are not exotic or rare, but necessary.

If you think about the friends in your life right now, you are likely to find at least one or two people whose relationships with you have the potential to develop beyond basic friendship: a sister, perhaps, who has been your best friend for life; your spouse, who started out as a fun date and over time became a soul mate; the woman from your book club, who always ends up talking to you about prayer and how to incorporate God into a busy life. Stop right there. Rewind. Replay. Those are your spiritual friends. That doesn't mean you can't and won't have more spiritual friends at different times and places in your life, but for now you can enjoy and nurture the special friendships that are often hidden in plain sight.

I have a friend I met about seven years ago, after I wrote my first book. She came to a talk I was giving at our local library. Then, a few months later, we ended up in the same babysitting co-op. We don't get to see each other very often because we are both busy writers and moms, but when we do get together for a movie or coffee, our talk always turns to God and prayer. We are clearly on parallel journeys, even though I am Catholic and she is Protestant. Doesn't matter. We are on a quest for a deeper spiritual path, one that is based on quiet meditation and spiritual reading. We are joined in spirit, if not in tradition.

When the movie *Into Great Silence* came out a couple of years ago, I couldn't find anyone who wanted to sit through three hours of almost complete silence at a movie theater. The film is a close-up look at the life of the Carthusian monks in the French Alps. There is no soundtrack, no plot, no dialogue—save for a few lines in French with subtitles. My husband looked at me as if I was crazy when I suggested he join me. So I called Robyn, certain that she would be game for something with a spiritual bent, no matter how long or intimidating. The two of us sat in the darkened theater taking in the peaceful and powerful scenes—and trying not to doze off in the silence as the clock ticked toward midnight.

On the drive home, we talked about the monks' vocations compared to our own, reflecting on our own callings as mothers, writers, and spiritual seekers. We talked about the complete lack of silence in our own busy lives and how we have to find a way to make our daily activities an ongoing prayer since we cannot retreat to the silence of a monastery. That is not a conversation I could have with just anyone, only with someone connected to me by something deeper than our similar jobs or home lives.

For me, my spiritual friendship with Robyn is one that manages to exist even though it is not continually fed. It is a friendship I am convinced will grow deeper as we each find more time in our lives outside of children and volunteer projects and work. For now it is enough that it is a spiritual touchstone. Robyn will e-mail me, talking about this or that. I will ask her how she can possibly manage to keep up a regular morning prayer schedule with three children clamoring for breakfast and all the things that need to be done before sending them off to school. We will trade spiritual books and sit through spiritual movies or talks. We didn't plan it or expect it. It blossomed naturally.

We rob ourselves of spiritual relationships when we assume that they require endless amounts of time and energy. The truth is that these friendships are often subtly present, sometimes even invisible, when life is going smoothly. Then, during times of crisis or struggle, they move to center stage and keep us steady.

Spiritual friendships have certain hallmarks, qualities that make them stand out. Those qualities will be explored at length in later chapters. For now, take a few minutes to reflect on the following questions in order to explore the spiritual friendships that may already exist in your life.

Food for Thought

1. Reflect on those deep friendships that have influenced your faith journey over the course of your lifetime. What, if anything, elevated these relationships to spiritual friendships?

2. If you are in a spiritual friendship today, how has that relationship made you a better person, not just spiritually but overall? How do you contribute to your friend's well-being?

3. Think about places where you can connect with other like-minded men and women who might want to share a spiritual friendship. Do you belong to a church community, a scripture study group, a knitting group or book club, a men's or women's association? Explore the possibilities.

Meditation

So often in our busy lives
we don't take the time to stop
and recognize the gifts in our midst—
the people with whom we share
special relationships, the friends who
make us stronger, kinder, gentler
through their own faith and compassion.
Today we give thanks for the friends
who are part of our lives and
for all those friends we have yet to meet.
May our hearts always be open to the
kindred spirit who wants to walk with us
on our spiritual journey, who shares our
love of God, who may become a companion,
a sounding board, a mentor, a soul friend.

Chapter 2

Acceptance:
Unconditional Love
in a Conditional World

*Do not ask me to abandon or forsake you! For wherever you go
I will go, wherever you lodge, I will lodge, your people shall be my
people, and your God my God.*

—Ruth 1:16

When my husband and I were married about fourteen years, we were contacted by the national
office of the Knights of Columbus to see if we
would be willing to be their featured "Valentine Couple"
on a website aimed at Catholic men. We just had to answer
some e-mail interview questions, which would be published
on the website. That seemed simple enough, but there was a
hitch. We had to answer the same questions separately—no
discussion beforehand, no peeking at each other's answers
after the fact. It was like a Catholic version of *The Newlywed
Game*. We could either come off smelling like roses or looking like fools.

Not being people who pass up challenges, we agreed.
The end result was incredibly affirming. Our answers were
so similar that some people might have thought that we
cheated. But we didn't. On one level, neither Dennis nor
I was surprised to learn that we were still so in sync with

17

each other. Maybe we were more in sync than ever. But to get a concrete affirmation of that was the greatest Valentine's gift I could ever receive. And in that one moment, I felt a glimmer of the unconditional love that every person hopes for in life.

I looked at my husband and my marriage with renewed hope and joy, realizing that unconditional love may not be easy. It may not even be possible, but sometimes we can come very close to that ideal—especially when God enters the picture. My husband, Dennis, put it best in one of his interview answers: "Mary and I have a strong marriage, but like all couples, we have had our disagreements and even serious fights. Without the commitment that comes with having God as the third person in that union, it is very easy to see how in a moment of anger, you might just throw it all away."

I loved that reference to God as the "third person in our marriage." It wasn't the first time I'd considered that, of course. But hearing my husband put it into words made it that much more powerful. It was a reminder that we can walk this road together as a couple, but if God doesn't have a central role in the relationship, it will be very hard to get through the tough times. Just as it is in marriage, so it is— perhaps to a slightly lesser degree—in spiritual friendship. Two friends trying to achieve an ideal relationship in a less-than-ideal world need to put God front and center to make that happen.

The Way of the World

Very few things in this world come without conditions. Our jobs, our homes, our health care, our hobbies, even our relationships typically come with at least a few strings attached. Most of us accept a life of conditions as part of the natural landscape of our daily existence. If we want our paychecks, we'd better do our jobs. If we hope to keep our houses, the mortgage payments had better be in the mail. If we want to keep up that friendship with the woman down the street, we had better join her book club. Most of us have reached a place where we understand, maybe without even consciously thinking about it, that nothing—not even friendship—is free.

Spiritual friendships, however, are truly unique. In fact, if spiritual friendships come with the usual strings attached, they aren't spiritual friendships. Obviously, spiritual friendships can't be completely and utterly unconditional because people are human, and we humans can't achieve perfection in this life. But spiritual friendships move far beyond what is found in our "everyday" friendships and acquaintances. It may seem idealistic or even impossible in our cynical society to imagine a friendship so true and deep, but the reality is that if God is placed at the center of a friendship, it can be transformed into something that goes far beyond the status quo. True spiritual friends are not looking out for themselves or for what they can gain from the relationship. They give from the heart, without tallying up anything that might be "owed" them. They go out of their way to "serve"—in the very best sense of the word—the person who holds this special place in their lives.

Pure and Perfect Love

When we talk about unconditional love in its purest form, we look to God. From the time we are children, we learn that God loves us without limits. We are created, loved, forgiven, adored by God in ways that are impossible for us to replicate exactly here on earth. And yet, we continue to desire that kind of pure love. We yearn for it.

St. Francis de Sales, the seventeenth-century bishop who wrote extensively about spiritual friendship, says that the kind of unconditional love we all crave has existed in its most perfect form since before time began in the relationship of the Holy Trinity. If there is one ultimate model of spiritual friendship, it is found in the relationship of the Father, Son, and Spirit. But what does that mean for those of us hoping to nurture a transcendent kind of love right here on earth? It means that even if we can never achieve a divine level of pure love, we still hold the Trinity up as the example of perfect friendship. The Trinity can teach us how to be more loving in our own relationships, much the same way Christ teaches us how to live the gospel without reservation.

"What is there to be loved and desired if friendship is not? And if friendship is to be loved and desired, what friendship can be so in comparison with that infinite friendship which is between the Father and Son . . ." St. Francis de Sales wrote in *Treatise on the Love of God*.[1]

You may be thinking that it *still* sounds too unrealistic to imagine, even for a moment, that mere mortals could have a friendship on par with the relationship between the three persons of the Trinity. And that's true. We cannot achieve an exact replica because we are not divine. But St. Francis de Sales explains that we can, in fact, find something of ourselves mirrored in that "infinite friendship" because we are made in God's image.

We have an "affinity of likeness," he says. There is a "correspondence between God and man" that allows us, maybe even propels us, to continually strive for the kind of spiritual perfection we see in our Creator.[2] That sounds poetic, but what does it mean for you and for me right here, right now?

Put into twenty-first-century terms, an "affinity of likeness" means simply that God created us in his image. Because of that, we have a need to seek him out as a model of pure love, to turn to him as an example of how to interact with those around us. A "correspondence" between God and humanity refers to the reciprocal relationship that exists between the Creator and the created: We are constantly drawn to God while God is constantly drawing us to him. We want God's love, and God wants to give us his love.

We turn to Father, Son, and Spirit again and again in an effort to get closer, to become more like the perfection we see there. For spiritual friends, the Trinity can offer a lesson in what it means, in a divine sense, to love without conditions, allowing us to translate that love into our human relationships as best we can. We see in the three persons of the Trinity an openness. The Father, Son, and Spirit are generous with one another and are in constant connection. And yet the three persons are distinct and separate from one another, never in danger of overtaking one another or suppressing one another. There is a harmony there that resonates with us. We want some piece of it for our own.

When we find a true spiritual friend, we can take what we see in the Trinity and apply it to our relationship in more modern and human ways. We can try to build a bond that is based not on power plays or pressure to conform, but is based instead on a deep love that overlooks petty differences that often derail an "average" friendship. Spiritual friends do not judge one another on worldly terms, but on God's terms. They do not fret over the little things that annoy or frustrate, but focus instead on the big picture. They offer each other guidance and support, maybe even a firm challenge if one or the other is going off in an unhealthy direction. But always the actions are based in love, not in anger or jealousy or manipulation.

Back to the Lesson Book

If you want to witness one of the most complete spiritual —and yet strictly mortal—friendships, simply open your bible to the very short Book of Ruth. There you will find the beautiful and inspiring story of Naomi and Ruth. Death and heartache form the backdrop of this book, but faith and self-sacrificing love are victorious.

Naomi and her husband, Elimelech, had moved from Bethlehem to the country of Moab nearby. Elimelech died, and his sons, Mahlon and Chilion, married Moabite women. Mahlon married Ruth, and Chilion married Orpah. When both of Naomi's sons died, Naomi decided to go back to Bethlehem and encouraged her daughters-in-law to go back to their own mothers and remarry. Orpah went reluctantly,

but Ruth, in what would become a passage that is memo-
rized, set to music, and read at weddings, replied: "Do not
ask me to abandon or forsake you! For wherever you go I
will go, wherever you lodge, I will lodge, your people shall
be my people, and your God my God" (Ru 1:16).

We may have heard this passage so many times that perhaps it's now simply part of our faith lexicon. But the reality
is that these brief but powerful lines present the essence of
unconditional love between spiritual friends. Although it is
often used to express marital love, the passage is about a
very different kind of the love—the love that exists between
friends centered in God. Yes, it can and should exist between
spouses as well, but it can also exist between people whose
bonds are not sacramental.

Once Naomi and Ruth returned to Bethlehem, Ruth
went to work in the barley fields to support herself and
her mother-in-law. Naomi, whose name meant "pleasant,"
told her people that they should now call her Mara, which
means "bitter." "I went away with abundance, and the Lord
made me destitute," she said (Ru 1:21). We can imagine that
Ruth, too, was burdened by her life.

Boaz, the owner of the fields and a relative of Naomi's
dead husband, was kind to Ruth because of her loyalty
to her mother-in-law. One night, Naomi sent Ruth to the
threshing floor with specific instructions that would remind
Boaz of his legal obligation to marry her and continue the
family line. Eventually, Boaz and Ruth did marry and have
a son named Obed. Obed was the father of Jesse, who was
the father of David, providing a link between Ruth and Jesus that is both literal and figurative. Ruth's redemption

through her marriage to Boaz parallels our own redemption through our spiritual marriage to Christ.[3]

This story may at first seem a little convoluted and complex, but the bottom line is plain and simple: spiritual friendship is not a one-way street; it is an endless loop of mutual care and concern.

In Naomi and Ruth, we see friends willing to sacrifice their own comforts and desires to benefit the other. It is the kind of sacrifice that, in a sense, mirrors what Jesus asks of all of us: to love another as ourselves and to be willing to lay down our very lives for a friend. In this Old Testament love between mother-in-law and daughter-in-law, we see a sacrifice so great that it rises to the level of redemption, leading both women closer to God. This story is not just about two nice people doing kind things for one another. It is about two women, bound by faith in God, doing what has to be done to move forward on their spiritual journeys. Spiritual friends—modern-day versions of Naomi and Ruth—can do the same thing on a less extreme level, pushing one another forward toward God.[4]

Most of us will not be asked to make the kinds of sacrifices that Ruth and Naomi made for each other, but we are still challenged as spiritual friends to be present and available, even during difficult times. It's not always easy, but it is a sign of spiritual growth and spiritual commitment when two friends can put aside things they may want for the greater good of the relationship and the end goal: God.

In the story of Naomi and Ruth, we see a shining example of what is possible when we focus our hearts, minds, and spirits on loving God and serving others. Suddenly—or maybe not so suddenly—our innate human inclination to protect and preserve our own well-being starts to open up in a way that reveals a softness, a generosity, a desire to give rather than to get.

What starts as a spark of a spiritual friendship can eventually develop into a fire of spiritual love. We begin, perhaps, as typical friends, and little by little, step by step, our friendship becomes infused with the fire of the Holy Spirit. What was once "just" an average friendship becomes something more because God has entered the scene in a real, maybe even radical, way. God's presence in friendship—much the way my husband described God's presence in our marriage—not only transforms the lives of the spiritual friends, but their interactions with their family, friends, and community as well. The spiritual fire radiates outward, enveloping others.

The Treasure in Our Midst

Spiritual friendships truly are gifts from God. We see the Spirit at work in our lives when we find ourselves in the midst of a happy "coincidence" that brings us face to face and heart to heart with someone who is clearly meant to walk with us on our spiritual journey—whether through phone calls and visits, shared prayers in silence, or much-needed laughter during a dinner out. Spiritual friends are complete friends, there through every mood and phase of our lives.

Margaret Robertson, sixty-one, remembers bumping into Brenda after daily morning Mass at their local suburban parish in New York back in the late 1990s. They would smile and say hello and then go about their days. Then they started talking. Soon the impromptu chats led to morning coffee, where the conversation often focused on matters of faith. The two became friends, and Brenda invited Margaret to join a women's club that raises money for local charities. There, Margaret met Cheryl and Mary Rita, women she recognized from church but didn't know. Before long a powerful little foursome of spiritual friends was developing. More than a decade later, it continues to grow stronger. Their faith and involvement in church provided common ground and a focal point for a friendship that quickly became more than any other friendships in their lives.

Whether they are calling each other to ask for prayers for family members and friends, traveling to Florida for a weekend getaway, or accompanying each other to doctor appointments or military send-offs, they are there for each other around the clock.

"There's always an element of God present," says Margaret, from simple things like saying grace before meals when they are on vacation together or sending one another spiritual bouquets, to more significant things like providing support when one member of the group is in crisis.

A few years ago, Mary Rita's daughter was in a car accident that left her near death. Things did not look good for the young woman, who was in a coma and had suffered a broken neck, among multiple serious injuries. The friends not only banded together through prayer, but also were physically present to Mary Rita, traveling to spend time in the hospital with her while she waited seemingly endless hours for her daughter's condition to improve. They also asked their pastor to celebrate a special Mass for the injured girl, taking on roles as lector and eucharistic ministers. Even Brenda, who was on vacation in Ireland at the time, went to a church there at the same time the Mass was being celebrated back in the States so that she could unite her prayers to those of her spiritual friends.

Margaret says unequivocally that there is nothing these friends wouldn't do for her. She knows that whatever help or support she might need, it will be there as soon as a word is uttered, sometimes even before. That is spiritual friendship of the highest order. These four women met because of their common faith journey. Their shared commitment to a deeper spiritual life has enabled their friendship to move from the superficial level that is typical of more pedestrian friendships to the profound place that is found at the heart of spiritual friendship.

"There's always a constant connection between us," says Margaret. "We don't always agree on every single aspect of spiritual life, but we are able to hear each other, and it doesn't stop us from being friends. We are all different, and we go to certain people in the group at certain times. We know each other's talents as well as understanding each other's spiritual sides. We help each other with all different things, but it's all interconnected. I can trust them implicitly."

Gift of Love

When I was younger, I would often say that the only person who ever loved me unconditionally was my mother. A little overly dramatic? Perhaps. Then again, that bond between parent and child is often the closest many of us ever get to the kind of unconditional love that rivals what we see in the Trinity. It is within the domestic church of our families that we first learn what it means to love without expecting anything in return, to love as God loves. At least that's how our families should work.

It's hard to pinpoint specifically what gave me that feeling of unconditional love in my relationship with my mother, but I think that's a fairly normal reaction. When we are loved so completely, we don't point to one single action or any particular conversation that demonstrates that love. Rather it is a way of life, a love that touches every aspect of our being. I think the fact that my mother's faith was so strong and that she devoted so much time to passing that faith on to me certainly played a significant role in our relationship and in the feelings she inspired.

She taught me about a loving God, and, in a sense, she mirrored that love in her relationship with me—strict but forgiving, strong but open. I really don't remember her yelling and punishing, and yet she garnered respect and affection not just from her children but from just about everyone she knew. By the time I was a young adult, my mother was not just my mother but my best friend as well. I was completely comfortable arguing points of faith with her. I knew I could disagree with her on something she considered non-negotiable. Even if her position on the matter remained unchanged, she would listen to my side and love me regardless of where the discussion ended. There was never a moment when I imagined something I did—or could do—would cut me off from that love in any permanent way.

That's what we're striving for when we talk about unconditional love within the boundaries of friendship, whether
it is between spouses or between parents and children or
between two strangers who have become friends. We may
disagree. We may even reach a place where something feels
big enough to destroy the bond, and yet we move through
it to find we have become closer, stronger in the face of
adversity.

Sometimes, when I am telling my son for the tenth time
to clean his room, I wonder if he feels that unconditional love
I felt when I was young. Am I adequately conveying to my
children on a day-to-day basis that, despite the expectations
and the nagging, the love I feel for them remains unchanged
and unconditional? Conversely, when my children seem to
be disobeying and disregarding almost everything I say, do I
remember that the sassiness or surliness are completely separate from the love they feel for me? Showing unconditional
love isn't easy, and sometimes accepting unconditional love
is even harder. We're human, after all, and we tend to expect
things of the people around us.

So, if it's difficult at times to adequately express such
deep and abiding love for our children or parents or spouses, how much more difficult is it to find that wellspring of
love within ourselves for a stranger-turned-friend? Many of
us can probably look to our spouses and see that what started as flirtation and romantic interest, slowly, maybe over
the course of years, changed into something deeper, spiritual. But can we build that kind of relationship with someone
with whom we share no blood ties or sacramental vows?

The answer to that question is as individual as every friendship. It has to come from the heart. Even if we recognize a friendship as one that has the potential to grow into something spiritual, it doesn't mean it will be easy. Then again, no relationship worth our time and devotion is ever easy. By grounding the relationship in God, however, it is *possible*. If we go back to the openness and generosity we see modeled in the Trinity, we can continue to strive for a friendship that is not based on personal gain or security or physical companionship, but on walking side by side, with God always in between.

From Friend to Spiritual Friend

When I first became friends with Bill, back in my post-college days, we had the typical office friendship—after-work outings with our coworkers, occasional trips to a play or to dinner. Both of us had found our vocations within the Church, Bill as a priest and me as a Catholic journalist. After each of us moved on from that particular office setting, we stayed in touch for a long time as we continued our work for the Church in different states, even different countries, and then we lost touch. Years later, Bill and I reconnected. Instead of get-togethers that involved traipsing around New York City, our renewed friendship shifted focus and began to encompass my entire family. When Dennis and I had our youngest child, Chiara, we asked Bill to be her godfather, knowing that this would be a role he would not only undertake with the utmost seriousness, but one that he would cherish.

What has happened in the three intervening years is remarkable to me. A friendship that was always solid and honest and fun has developed into one that is also spiritual and deep and, yes, unconditional. Although it didn't happen all at once, over the past few years Bill and I have moved from being friends who simply chat about work or current events to friends who talk about our journeys toward God. On the phone and during visits, we discuss our vocations and our spiritual goals and struggles. It has become clear to both of us that this friendship is meant to take us further down our respective paths. It really is a blessing, and the unconditional aspect is especially grace-filled in that I have come to realize that it extends not only to me but also to my family.

When I look back and see the signposts that led this friendship in new directions, it's not surprising that the most monumental event in that transformation was a sacrament. The baptism of Chiara had a powerful impact on our friendship because it signified a certain trust on my part and a certain willingness on Bill's. That, I believe, was the Spirit at work. Now, three years later, it is an unspoken but acknowledged fact that each of us is available to the other. Although we live three hours apart and both have busy lives, we know we can count on one another in times of difficulty and need as well as times of joy and celebration. When Bill's father died, I knew I had to do what was necessary to get to the funeral. When my older daughter, Olivia, made her first Communion, Bill was there not just as a friend but also as the priest who gave her first eucharist.

What happened in my friendship with Bill is not unlike what often happens in any spiritual friendship as it grows and develops. Spiritual friendships don't always start off in a strictly spiritual way. Instead, they often develop over time from something typical to something verging on mystical. But even in those spiritual friendships that do not start out with an obvious spiritual focus, God is always present. God may be on the periphery at first, but he remains the common thread that binds the fabric of the friendship together. God is the one necessary ingredient.

Food for Thought

1. Reflect for a moment on the relationships in your life that have been unconditional, or close to it—from parents and children to spouses and siblings to friends with no blood ties. How have these relationships impacted your life in general and your spiritual life in particular?

2. When you think about the ultimate models of spiritual friendship we've discussed in this chapter—the Trinity, Ruth and Naomi—how do you see them as a way to inform and guide your own spiritual friendships?

3. Consider the relationships in your life that have the potential to blossom into truly spiritual friendships. How might you be able to nurture these friendships and strengthen your spiritual ties?

Meditation

In our cynical, me-first world
it's easy to imagine that unconditional love
is just a fantasy or a relic of days gone by.
But unconditional love is real,
something that can exist in our lives,
if we are willing to get out of our own way
and welcome into our hearts those friends
whose love comes without requirements,
who give without expecting a return.
Today we reflect on those times
when we have felt loved unconditionally
and when we have loved another so completely.
This is how our God loves each one of us.
We pray now to always be aware of that love
and to share it with the friends who enter our lives
when we least expect them but most need them.

Chapter 3

Love of God:
The Common Thread

What is a friend? A single soul dwelling in two bodies.
—Aristotle

When I was in high school, my parish's Catholic Youth Organization was at the center of both my social and my spiritual life. For those of us at the core of the group, our parish was a second home. We planned liturgies together, right down to baking our own Communion hosts under the watchful eye of my mother in our suburban kitchen. We ran car washes to raise funds for conventions and trips. We sang at a nursing home each month, learning classic songs like "Bicycle Built for Two" and "Heart of My Heart" so the old folks could sing along.

CYO was an oasis in the desert of adolescence, giving all of us a safe place to grow and laugh and get to know ourselves without the usual peer pressure or isolation we often found in the halls of high school. At just about every CYO liturgy or celebration, our folk group sang a song called "My Friend." I don't recall all of the lyrics, but the general gist was that my friend was "half of my soul," someone to help us be our own best selves. That song was a favorite, to be sure. There was something powerful about the idea that even during this difficult stage of life, we had found true friends to talk with us, laugh with us, cry with us, walk with us—no matter what.

That may sound simplistic at first, but it really does define what spiritual friendship is about and what pushes a "normal" friendship to spiritual heights. For those of us in CYO back in the late '70s, this song about friendship summed up for us what we had found in the shelter of our parish gymnasium—a group of other like-minded teenagers who were bucking the typical teenage trends. We were at different stages of adolescence, from different schools and different backgrounds. But in that group we had a common focus: God. In that group, we began to realize that we were not alone after all. And that is one of the great gifts of spiritual friendship, no matter what your age.

When we stop for a moment and look at our lives, we can probably rattle off a fairly long list of friends. They may be people we know from work, parents of our children's friends, members of our church choir, the women who take aerobics with us at the gym. Those are all good friends to have. These are the kinds of friends who round out our lives, people we meet for coffee, people who share our parenting concerns, people who may like the same kind of music or movies or who may enjoy getting together to knit or bowl. And yet, these are not necessarily spiritual friends. Spiritual friends don't just share our love of jazz music or antiquing. Spiritual friends share our love of God.

Learning from the Experts

St. Francis de Sales wrote about spiritual friendship more than four hundred years ago. His insights and wisdom are as relevant today as they were when he first shared them. He explained spiritual friendship like this in his classic *Introduction to the Devout Life*: "if the bond of your mutual liking be charity, devotion, and Christian perfection, God knows how very precious a friendship it is! Precious because it comes from God, because it tends to God, because God is the link that binds you, because it will last forever in Him. Truly it is a blessed thing to love on earth as we hope to love in Heaven, and to begin that friendship here which is to endure forever there."[1]

St. Francis went on to say that he was not talking about the kind of love "due all mankind," but of a spiritual friendship that "binds souls together," one that leads them to "share devotions and spiritual interests, so as to have but one mind between them."[2]

Once again, the masters of spiritual friendship leave us wondering if such a deep and personal connection is attainable in our high-tech, low-touch world. To have "one mind" with a friend? Can we ever hope to experience such a thing? Well, St. Francis didn't just write about it; he lived it. His letters of spiritual direction display the deep friendships he nurtured in his own life, none more extraordinary than the friendship he shared with St. Jane de Chantal.

In his preface to *Francis de Sales, Jane de Chantal: Letters of Spiritual Direction*, the renowned theologian Henri J. M. Nouwen wrote that the "Jesus-centered friendship" of Francis and Jane challenges all of us. "Without Jesus, friends tend to become possessive of each other. . . . With Jesus there remains ample freedom for the unique ways of the individual persons. Without Jesus, friends tend to close in on each other and ignore the larger world. With Jesus friendships can bear fruit which many can enjoy. Francis and Jane show us clearly that the deepest intimacy among people is an intimacy that finds its origin and goal not in human partners, but in God who gives people to each other in friendship to be incarnate manifestations of the divine love," Nouwen wrote.[3]

Certainly we see that sentiment was central to the lives of Francis and Jane, in the spiritual goals they achieved in their lifetimes, and in the spiritual influence they continue to have to this day. Their letters to each other (although most of Jane's letters to Francis were destroyed) display a deep affection. From the tone of their letters, it is easy to see that in the wrong hands, this friendship could have become an inward-moving affection that could have isolated these friends in self-serving ways. Devoid of God, such a friendship could have become narcissistic. The two friends could have focused solely on each other and might have allowed their friendship to evolve into an unhealthy attachment rather than a true friendship.

Instead, what we witness between Francis and Jane, in true spiritual friend form, is an affection that expanded outward. Their love for each other and their influence on each other's spiritual journey extended into the world around them, engulfing others in its reach. That is evident in the numerous letters they wrote not only to each other, but also in the letters of spiritual direction they wrote to the many friends who sought their counsel. Centuries later, the power of their friendship is still evident, as modern men and women look to them as models of what spiritual friends can achieve when God remains at the center of a relationship.

Spiritual friendship is not about giving up our individuality and taking on the traits of our friends. It is not about changing ourselves to conform to the other person's likes or dislikes or about suppressing feelings or opinions to benefit the other. It is about honesty, about two people walking on separate but parallel paths together. We walk alongside each other, living our own lives, proceeding with whatever we are called to do as individuals. But then, maybe once a day or once a week or once a year, we come together to gather strength from each other and refocus our spiritual journey.

Francis and Jane went for long periods without actually seeing each other, but their letters kept them connected. The letters fed their spiritual lives and pushed them further along the path to God. The result was a friendship that led to them not only doing amazing things in partnership with each other, but also to accomplish amazing things as individuals. Perhaps that is why their story continues to inspire others to seek out their wisdom and follow their example.

A Spiritual Friendship Unfolds

Francis de Sales, who was born in 1567, did not meet Jane de Chantal until 1604, the same year he became Bishop of Geneva. Jane, a widow and the mother of four young children, went to Dijon to hear Francis preach a series of Lenten sermons. In the years of grief following her husband's death, Jane felt the stirrings of a religious vocation. Francis became her spiritual director, but their relationship soon evolved into one of mutual spiritual support and guidance. They formed a lifelong friendship that resulted in their collaboration in the founding of a religious congregation for women. They founded the Congregation of the Visitation of Holy Mary in 1610 in Savoy. This congregation allowed Jane, and other widows, to pursue their religious vocations while fulfilling their responsibilities as mothers and daughters. Francis died in 1622. Jane, who later received spiritual direction from St. Vincent de Paul, continued the mission she began with St. Francis de Sales until her death in 1641.

Francis and Jane's friendship demonstrates several critical things: It is possible for a man and woman to share a platonic but deeply spiritual relationship. It is possible for a cleric and a layperson to develop a spiritual friendship that is not simply a "one-way" relationship, with the cleric always in the "directing" role. It is possible to nurture a spiritual friendship from great distances with very little personal contact.

"God gave me a tremendous love for your soul. As you became more and more open with me, a marvelous obligation arose for my soul to love yours more and more; that's why I was prompted to write to you that God had given me to you," Francis wrote to Jane in 1604. "I didn't believe that anything could be added to the affection I felt for you, especially when I was praying for you. But now, my dear daughter, a new quality has been added—I don't know what to call it. All I can say is that its effect is a great inner delight which I feel whenever I wish you perfect love of God and other spiritual blessings."[4]

Francis continued to talk about how affections differ from one relationship to the next, but that there was a "certain something" in his relationship with Jane that was "extremely good for me."[5] Once again we see the heart of spiritual friendship exposed. Spiritual friends are good for one another, even when they can't quite put their fingers on the "certain something" that makes them so. Spiritual friendships lead the friends in right paths, strengthening each of the individuals but also strengthening relationships that exist outside the orbit of the spiritual friendship.

Not an Exclusive Club

Francis and Jane show us that spiritual friendship cannot and should not be narrowly focused on only the two main people involved. Each of them had multiple spiritual friends with whom they shared long letters of direction and support. However, the relationship that existed between Francis and Jane was the most vibrant and vital of all their spiritual friendships. It was the friendship that gave them strength in their own spiritual struggles and at the same time nourished all their other friendships. In Francis and Jane we see the complete commitment and devotion that is so crucial to spiritual friendship as well as the complete openness to others that must go hand-in-hand with it.

Spiritual friendship is always about inclusion and expansion, never about isolation. If our goal is a deeper relationship with God, it is inevitable that our Jesus-centered lives will encourage us to cast an ever-wider net in order to bring others into the spiritual friendship fold. And yet, it is possible we will find that one spiritual friend who stands out among the rest. Like Francis and Jane, we may discover one person who is so keenly attuned to our spiritual thoughts and needs that the relationship rises above all other friendships. C. S. Lewis, who wrote about friendship in his book *The Four Loves*, says that when true friends first discover each other, it is as if they are taken by surprise, realizing for the first time that they are not the only ones who feel a particular way or desire a particular thing.

"Friendship arises out of mere companionship when two or more of the companions discover that they have in common some insight or interest or even taste which the others do not share and, which, till that moment, each believed to be his own unique treasure (or burden)," Lewis wrote in *The Four Loves*, which also covers the love associated with affection, eros, and charity.[6]

Lewis focused on the necessity of friendship and the fact that it is undervalued and misunderstood by modern society. He said that friendship is too often seen as a "diversion," something "marginal." Friendship today is not viewed as a "main course in life's banquet," as it once was.[7] "To the ancients, friendship seemed the happiest and most fully human of all loves: the crown of life and the school of virtue. The modern world, in comparison, ignores it," Lewis writes.[8]

Lewis shared a deep friendship with author J. R. R. Tolkien, who was instrumental in Lewis's conversion to Christianity. These authors met at Magdalen College at Oxford University and later influenced each other's writings and spirituality. In fact, it has been said that we would not have Lewis's *The Chronicles of Narnia* or Tolkien's *The Lord of the Rings* if the two had not met and encouraged each other in their efforts to transmit gospel truth through fantasy fiction.

"The unpayable debt that I owe to [Lewis] was not 'influence' as it is ordinarily understood but sheer encouragement," Tolkien said. "He was for long my only audience. Only from him did I ever get the idea that my 'stuff' could be more than a private hobby. But for his interest and unceasing eagerness for more I should never have brought *The L[ord] of the R[ings]* to a conclusion. . . ."[9]

In turn, Lewis, in *The Four Loves,* described the power of his own friendship with Tolkien and their other mutual friends: "In a perfect friendship this appreciative love is, I think, often so great and so firmly based that each member of the circle feels, in his secret heart, humbled before all the rest. . . . Those are golden sessions; when four or five of us after a hard day's walking have come to our inn; when our slippers are on, our feet spread out towards the blaze and our drinks at our elbows; when the whole world, and something beyond the world, opens itself to our minds as we talk."[10]

The relationship between Lewis and Tolkien was not simply a matter of common interest or professional pedigree, but of a common desire to use their talents to deepen their own faith and share it with others.

In *The Four Loves,* Lewis explained that what our modern world classified as "friendships" are often merely "acquaintanceships" and not the stuff of real friendships. And that, Lewis concluded, is because few people experience the kind of friendships that occur on a soul-to-soul level, the kind he shared with Tolkien. Acquaintances might share a love of sports, art, or reading, but real friends join us in a deeper kind of activity.

"The friends will be doing something together, but something more inward . . . still collaborating, but in some work the world does not, or not yet, take account of; still traveling companions, but on a different kind of journey," Lewis wrote. "Hence we picture lovers face to face but friends side by side; their eyes look ahead."[11]

Side by Side

For those of us longing to move farther down the path toward God, the idea of having a spiritual friend standing at our side and looking out at the same goal is comforting in so many ways. It means we will have company on our journey. It means that even though the rest of the world doesn't always understand our hunger, at least one other person does. It means, as Lewis notes, that we are not alone, and that is a powerful thing.

Being on a spiritual journey is a challenge, but to be on that journey in isolation can be devastating to our spiritual growth. We need friends who will open their hearts to us, as Jane did with Francis, and who will listen to our innermost thoughts without judgment or ridicule or indifference.

St. Francis de Sales, in *Introduction to the Devout Life*, talks about the need for spiritual friendship, saying, "those who aim at a devout life require to be united one with another by a holy friendship, which excites, stimulates, and encourages them in well-doing."[12]

More simply put, friendship isn't a luxury but one of the basic necessities of spiritual life, much like food and water are basic to our physical lives. Without spiritual friendship, the journey toward God becomes much more difficult. Think about those times in your life when you really needed someone to talk to or someone to sit with you in silence. There may have been times when you found yourself in a spiritual crisis, wondering where God was or what you were supposed to learn from a particular cross. Maybe it was the loss of a job or an illness, or perhaps an emotional struggle with a child. Maybe it was a falling out with a family member or friend, or a financial crisis that threatened our security.

It is during difficult times like these that true friends are indispensable. They often provide basic needs—meals for the family, rides to the doctor, babysitting during appointments. But, even more important, they provide for the more ethereal needs as well—prayers, handholding, hugs, long walks together, notes thoughtfully written.

When I had a miscarriage years ago, it was a particularly difficult time. Because of the circumstances surrounding the miscarriage, I had to have weekly blood tests for an entire year. It was a constant reminder of my loss, and of the fact that my own life might be in danger if those blood counts went in the wrong direction. My husband did all that he could to help me through it, but he, too, was suffering his own grief from the loss of our unborn child.

Many friends and relatives sent cards and flowers, all of them well-meaning. But I remember how a few of those cards made me feel worse. They took a "you're-through-the-worst-of-it" approach, when, in my mind and heart, I was not even close to being through the worst of it. Then, without being asked, a few friends recognized my struggle and made a monumental difference. One brought a lovingly prepared homemade dinner and fresh-cut flowers from her garden. Another friend, who had also suffered a miscarriage, brought words of comfort and real-life experience that helped me see the light at the end of my dark tunnel. Another work friend sent a beautiful and delicate orchid with a note telling me about the loss of her son and the grief she knew I was feeling.

Through their kind words and generous gifts, I found the strength I needed to pull myself out of my sadness and fear so that I could turn my attention back to my one-year-old son and my husband and a hopeful future.

We all experience times in our lives when we need the wisdom and love of friends who know us best, or friends who have shared similar experiences. We need each other, not in a co-dependent, anxious sort of way, but in a balanced, God-centered way. Whether we are in crisis or just trying to get through a regular day, we need people who understand us. We need people with whom we can share one heart, and, as St. Francis de Sales suggested, one mind. All other friendships, he said, are "but as a shadow" of what we find in true spiritual friendship.[13]

Our true friends know us and know how to care for us—often without saying a word. These are friendships to celebrate, nurture, and protect. These are friendships that will—in the words of my old CYO song—help us to be our own best selves. They challenge us to dig deep into our

souls and to reach out and touch the souls of others through
our words and actions.

Food for Thought

1. Reflect on the deep friendship that St. Francis de Sales
   shared with St. Jane de Chantal. How do your deepest
   friendships lead you forward on your spiritual journey
   and inspire you to take on new challenges?

2. Think about those friends who share your love of
   God and your desire to make spiritual "progress."
   How might you build on those existing friendships to
   provide support and encouragement to one another on
   a regular basis?

3. Spiritual friends don't necessarily face each other.
   Instead, they look outward at the same goal, side by
   side. What goals are you and your spiritual friends
   facing together? What can you do to work toward
   those goals in partnership?

Meditation

As spiritual friends,
we are bound together by God,
the common thread woven into
the fabric of our individual lives.
God is the rudder that steers
our friendships on right paths,
the shining light that leads us
even in our darkest moments.
Today we celebrate the blessing
of friends who see into our souls,

know our hearts, share our yearnings.
Together we will seek the joy
that comes from living a life
grounded in something greater than
what this world has to offer.

Chapter 4

Humility, Honesty, and Charity:

A Perfect Storm of Virtues

Put on then, as God's chosen ones, holy and beloved, heartfelt
compassion, kindness, humility, gentleness, and patience, bearing
with one another and forgiving one another, if one has a grievance
against another; as the Lord has forgiven you, so must you also do.
And over all these put on love, that is, the bond of perfection.

—Colossians 3:12–14

On October 4, 1976, on the Feast of St. Francis, Walt
Chura opened Simple Gifts, a Catholic Worker
bookstore in Albany, New York. The bookstore
was more than a just a place to shop. It was a place where
people would share a cup of coffee and some conversation.
Walt became friends with spiritual seekers from all walks
of life—some Christian and some not. Patrons and visitors
even included a Jewish Sufi, a Jewish atheist, and one loy-
al supporter—a Presbyterian minister—who kept coming
back to Simple Gifts for more than thirty years.

When Dan Wheeler first started visiting Simple Gifts,
he was pastoring two churches in New York's Capital Region. He would routinely come in, get some coffee, and talk
with Walt about issues that the Catholic Worker bookstore
was always trying to promote—peace, justice, nonviolence,

caring for the earth. The two men were drawn together right off the bat, not only because of common interests but because of shared personal connections. They knew many of the same people, moved in the same circles.

The friendship grew from that common ground.

"Although we come from quite different ecclesial traditions, we had a lot in common in terms of social values and spiritual values," says Walt, who is a Secular Franciscan and heads the Thomas Merton Society of the Capital Region. "Part of what drew us together was a contemplative kind of spirit. I was trying, in the Catholic Worker tradition, to promote and practice a life that was a balance of contemplation and action."

Walt learned that Dan and his family had a history of taking in homeless people and allowing them to live in their home as part of their family. It was an act of charity completely in tune with one Catholic Worker mission— providing hospitality to the homeless.

"That was very dear to my heart. It was the engine that increased our attraction to one another," says Walt, who explains that the friendship soon grew to include their wives and children. "Our families are very much intertwined. We shared cares and burdens. . . . When you share one another's burdens, you get real close."

For years, Walt and Dan have met every Thursday morning for a two-hour breakfast where they talk about what is going on in their personal and spiritual lives. "We do a lot of mutual spiritual direction," explained Walt, adding that through his influence, Dan became interested in Thomas Merton and went on retreat with Walt to the Abbey of Gethsemani in Trappist, Kentucky. Conversely, Dan encouraged Walt to study scripture in a more intense way.

"I know we both feel that we are closer to each other than we are to our own blood brothers because of our spiritual connection," Walt said. "What we have is on a different level, on a different plane—a spiritual plane."

Walt and Dan portray a modern spiritual friendship at its best. In them, we see a critical quality that is at the heart of all true spiritual friendships: virtue. But what exactly is virtue?

When we think of virtuous people, we often think of saints in heaven, knights in shining armor, or people in morally and spiritually high places. But virtue is—or can be—part of ordinary lives too. Whether we realize it or not, the ways we treat the person ahead of us in line at the grocery store or the coworker in a board meeting or a sick relative at the hospital are all opportunities to make virtue real in practical ways. Virtue is basically a habit of doing good.

When it comes to spiritual friendship, virtue is front and center. Spiritual friends magnify our virtuous qualities. More casual friends might bring out the worst in us through competitiveness, idle gossip, jealousy. Spiritual friends, however, bring out the best—in inspiring us to live in humility, honesty, charity. Spiritual friends inspire us to move beyond pettiness to a place where our hearts and minds are focused on doing what is right.

That's not to say that there won't be times in even the best spiritual friendships when we might feel those "normal" tendencies creeping in. Walt says that he and Dan sometimes get into "heated conversations" about particular things. But because of the strength and depth and character of spiritual friendship, those moments are more likely to be times of growth than times of anxiety or negativity. In the company of a soul mate, we put aside anger in favor of empathy, judgment in favor of humility. We begin to respond as Christ would.

Side by side with a spiritual friend, we are able to apply the lofty virtues of faith, hope, and charity. Perhaps we do it by talking out our struggles over coffee. Maybe we do it by working side by side on a Habitat for Humanity building project. Or perhaps we do it kneeling together at a prayer vigil for peace in front of our church each week. On the surface, virtue can seem so ethereal and indescribable. But it becomes a practical reality when spiritual friends allow their relationship to take root and grow.

In the Letter of St. Paul to the Colossians quoted at the beginning of this chapter, we see what is essentially the definition of a spiritual friendship. It is a "bond of perfection" that is built on love, above all else. Yes, the essential elements of compassion and honesty, humility and patience must be present as well, but love reigns supreme. If this deep love is present and pure and true, the friends are able to forge a "bond of perfection" that draws them ever closer to God and to each other.

It might be tempting to suggest that St. Paul's counsel about Christian friendship is simply not realistic in our modern world. In fact, Paul's directive to the earliest Christian communities is still very much relevant to our own lives centuries later. After all, what are small Christian communities if not bands of spiritual friends focused on living

Christ's message of love? In St. Paul's "bond of perfection," we see that the deep roots of spiritual friendship are grounded, before anything else, in God and in the gospel. Spiritual friendship is not just about finding like-minded companions; it is about building God-centered relationships that will bring Jesus' message of mercy and compassion, love and forgiveness out into the greater world.

In his Letter to the Ephesians, Paul sets up a similar model of how Christians are to treat one another and live their communal lives. This, of course, has everything to do with how spiritual friends treat one another. Paul suggested that they should "live a life worthy of the calling you have received, with perfect humility, meekness, and patience, bearing with one another lovingly. Make every effort to preserve the unity which has the Spirit as its binding force" (Eph 4:1–3).

Again, we see held up the simple yet hard-to-live-out qualities of meekness, patience, and humility. Humility, a virtue that serves as the foundation for all the others, is not an easy thing to grasp in our modern world. It has a self-defeating ring to it. Too often we associate the word "humility" with "humiliation." Humility, as lived out, involves surrendering ourselves to God and to our brothers and sisters in Christ in order to serve as Christ served, to love as Christ loved.

In one of his letters to St. Jane de Chantal, St. Francis de Sales wrote: "It is not necessary to be always and at every moment attentive to all the virtues in order to practice them; that would twist and encumber your thoughts and feelings too much. Humility and charity are the master ropes; all the others are attached to them. We need only hold on to these two: one is at the very bottom and the other at the very top. The preservation of the whole building depends on its foundation and its roof. We do not encounter much difficulty in practicing other virtues if we keep our heart bound to the practice of these two. They are the mother virtues."[1]

But what does that mean? How do we practice humility and charity in our spiritual friendships and in our lives?

It's clear that these virtues were pivotal in friendship between Walt and Dan. Their relationship spurred them on in their work among the poor and living out the Franciscan-Catholic Worker ideals in a secular world. Their different backgrounds and different faiths also provided many opportunities for them to practice charity and humility.

Walt talked about Dan's "great appreciation for the eucharist" and how it kept the two friends closer. "We have had conversations about the nature of the eucharist, and we know how far each of us can go. But we can go far enough together that it's not a point of conflict. It's realizing how much we are both drawn to the eucharist," Walt said, explaining that there have been many times over the years when the two friends have not had identical views on deeply personal and important matters.

As close as these friends were, there were issues where they could not agree, places where they could not stand together. It took humility to recognize those differences. It took charity to avoid conflict and alienation. The opposite of humility is pride, and there is really no place for pride in spiritual friendship.

That doesn't mean that your beliefs and ideas matter less than your friend's. It just means that you must respect your spiritual friend and his or her position on various issues. You can't get caught up in the idea that you're always right. Give and take is the key here. Listening and talking, talking and listening. Always being open to the thoughts and needs of this person whose soul is linked to yours is fundamental. And your spiritual friend should be approaching you in a similar fashion, with the same humility and charity, honesty and compassion.

St. Paul offered further teaching about virtue-based friendships. In his Letter to the Philippians, he wrote: "Never act out of rivalry or conceit; rather, let all parties think humbly of others as superior to themselves, each of you looking to others' interests rather than to his own. Your attitude must be that of Christ: 'Though he was in the form of God, he did not deem equality with God something to be grasped at. Rather, he emptied himself and took the form of a slave, being born in the likeness of men. He was known to be of human estate, and it was thus that he humbled himself, obediently accepting even death, death on a cross!'" (Phil 2:4–8).

Friendship with God

When St. Paul talked about true friendship and virtue, he led us back to Christ, where our best and deepest spiritual friendship must exist. We may have many earthly spiritual friends in our lives. Always at the center of those friendships must be our spiritual friendship with the one who made us, the one who patiently waits for us to recognize and welcome him.

Some time ago, I went on a silent weekend retreat in the Adirondack Mountains of upstate New York. It was my first silent retreat, and I was scared to go because it seemed so incredibly intense. No talking, no writing, no reading, and no "casual eye contact." They might as well have said, "No breathing." I am a talker and a writer and a reader and the kind of person who strikes up casual conversations with the bagger at the grocery store, the librarian at the checkout desk, and the woman on the mat next to me in yoga class. How would I go for two whole days without talking, even at meals? But I felt a calling, an urge to go and spend quiet time with God. Time for silence was something I never found time for in the midst of my busy life at home.

I arrived at the rustic mountain retreat center not knowing anyone and not knowing what to expect. After the evening meal, we introduced ourselves and learned a little bit about how our weekend would work. Then, we entered into the silence during Compline and meditation. It felt easy at first because it was late in the day. It was dark, and silence seemed appropriate.

But on the following morning when our director rang a "bell of mindfulness" at 6:30 a.m., we were "called" down to *Lectio Divina* and a silent breakfast. Sitting across the table from someone, eating my oatmeal and not speaking was one of the hardest things I've ever done in my spiritual practice. And yet, I found that if I focused on my food and became mindful of how I was eating and the gift of the new day from God, an awkwardness disappeared, and I was able to let go of my self-conscious feelings and go a little bit deeper into this silent, sacred place I was creating in my mind and soul.

Throughout the weekend, the silence became easier to accept. That was the reverse of what I expected. I walked slowly through the woods, thinking about every step, every scurrying newt that crossed my path, every rustle of tree limbs. When the rain started to fall gently on the lake, I sat in a little lean-to and stared out at the water, letting my rushing thoughts float by like leaves on the lake. It was peaceful. It was sacred. It was the first opportunity I'd had in a long time to spend some quality time with God.

That night, as I fell asleep in my room in the glow of my battery-powered candle, I could hear not only the noises of the forest and the wind rustling in the trees, but the sound of distant drumbeats. The "Connecting to the Earth" retreat was just through the woods. I loved knowing that there was another group of people out there who were trying to find spiritual space and renewal in their own way. It was a powerful reminder of our interconnectedness even when our paths are completely different.

In the morning, I could hear the soft sound of flute music drifting through the trees from the Earth Connection's campsite. Sitting in an Adirondack chair, staring off at the clouds hanging just above the lake, listening to the somber notes of the flute in the distance was like living in a dream. So peaceful, so spiritual, so filled with the majesty and wonder of God and all creation.

When Sunday morning arrived, I didn't want to break the silence. In the silence, I had found an invitation to deepen my relationship with God, to take it in a new direction, one that moves away from my needs and desires to a place of peaceful surrender. In my daily action-packed life, I made little time for building a relationship with God, who should be my first friend among friends. But there by a crystal clear lake in the mountains, with God's magnificence all around me, it became obvious that my calling is not simply to pray to God and wait for a response, but to build a friendship with God. I want to see my Creator as someone with whom I can just sit in silence, like a lifelong friend, who requires no entertainment, no busy chatter, no affectations.

That retreat experience reverberated in my "regular" life when I returned home. I found myself eating more slowly and mindfully, seeking out silence in the middle of the chaos. I found myself better equipped to truly open myself up to my spiritual friends in a way that was unselfish. Rather than wanting to focus on my struggles, my needs, I was more willing to focus on the needs of someone else. That is the fruit of building a friendship with God first and letting it shape the friendships we have with others.

Jesus spoke of this kind of deep and altruistic friendship when he told his disciples: "This is my commandment: love one another as I have loved you. There is no greater love than this: to lay down one's life for one's friends. You are my friends if you do what I command you. I no longer speak of you as slaves, for a slave does not know what his master is about. Instead I call you friends, since I have made known to you all that I heard from my Father" (Jn 15:12–15).

Jesus is our friend. God is our friend. Often we don't see God in that role. We see him off in the distance, perhaps as a parent figure or a protector. But it can really help our earthly spiritual friendships if we can learn to focus in on God as friend, companion, comforter, listener—all those things we look for in a true friend. By nurturing this most essential spiritual friendship, perhaps in a few minutes of silence each day, we begin to see the shape our earthly friendships must take.

I recall that my young daughter was once crying because she had done something she thought would upset me. After talking with her for a little while, I hugged her and said, "There is nothing you can say or do that will ever make me love you less. I will love you for all time, no matter what." And after I said it, I felt my own shoulder relax as I realized that this is how God feels about us. No matter how many mistakes we make, no matter how many times we choose the wrong thing, he loves us. What a powerful and comforting thought. We need to take that bond of love, that bond of perfection, and build it into our spiritual friendships. Allow them to mirror the friendship we have with God, filled with unconditional love that cannot be shaken by mistakes or arguments.

Once we develop, or begin to develop, a deep friendship with God, we can use our experience to initiate or nurture spiritual friendships with those who share our hunger for a deeper faith life. Perhaps we want to nurture a friendship with someone from church or work, with a sibling or parent or child. Without the God connection, friendships can easily slip into the typical relationships we see in our world today—temporary, surface level, replaceable. By anchoring our earthly friendships to our heavenly friendship with

God, we add a dimension that is not easily shaken by the ways of the world around us. God becomes a touch point, constantly bringing us back to a virtue-centered life and virtue-centered friendships.

Perhaps you belong to a prayer group or a scripture study group or a yoga class or knitting club where you are drawn to one or two of the other participants. Maybe you always seem to end up talking about spiritual issues, and it's clear that even if you don't share the same faith, you do share the same desire to take your spirituality to a new level. In pursuing the friendship, things can go one of two ways. You can stick to the more superficial side of things, talking about the latest movies you've seen and your vacation plans and sharing a cup of coffee. Or you can approach this from a completely different direction, starting instead with your common spiritual bond and consciously building on it. Talk about spiritual books you may be reading, discuss struggles you may be having in your prayer life or faith life in general, set a date to visit a spiritual spot or attend a spiritual lecture or retreat together. Look for ways to make the friendship God-focused. In doing that, you move the friendship away from the more worldly habits that friends can sometimes get caught up in—gossip, consumerism, jealousy, pettiness, annoyance over minor differences. With God at its center, the friendship leans toward virtue. There is a natural inclination to be charitable and humble, honest and caring. Even when you disagree with your friend, you find kind ways to express your opinion without harshness or judgment or anger.

Pay It Forward

When it comes to a virtue-centered spiritual friendship, nothing is as critical as humility. This is not about false humility, about building up another person just to make him feel good or to make ourselves feel magnanimous. This is about true humility. But what is *true* humility?

St. Francis de Sales, in *Introduction to the Devout Life*, explains it like this: "Humility drives Satan away, and cherishes the gifts and graces of the Holy Spirit within us, and for that reason all the Saints—and especially the King of Saints and His Blessed Mother—have always esteemed the grace of humility above all other virtues."[2]

Francis went on to say that exterior humility is when men and women put aside the "vainglory" of the world, that temptation to hold themselves in high esteem and pride themselves on the way they look or the job they hold or the clothes they wear. Interior humility, on the other hand, is a recognition of the great gifts God has given us and of our utter dependence on him. When we bring this kind of humility into our relationships, we can elevate friendship to spiritual friendship.

"If men share false and vain things, their friendship will be false and vain; if that which is good and true, their friendship will be good and true, and the better that which is the staple of the bond, so much the better will the friendship be. That honey is best which is culled from the choicest flowers, and so friendship built upon the highest and purest intercommunion is the best," St. Francis de Sales wrote.[3]

So we start with humility, which does not mean we cast our eyes downward and act as if we are lower than others. It means we put the needs of our spiritual friends first. We recognize that all we have comes from God and that we would be nothing without God. This foundation of God-centered self-understanding leads naturally then to the other key virtues of spiritual friendship: honesty, patience, kindness, empathy, charity. These are the things that distinguish spiritual friendships from what Francis de Sales called "false" or "frivolous" friendships that are grounded in worldly things.

St. Francis de Sales was careful to point out the dangers of false friendships, and some of those should be noted at this point because if a friendship isn't virtuous, it could be more harmful than good. Anything that is founded on "sensuality, vanity, or frivolity" is not worthy of the name "friendship," he said, adding that relationships based on good looks, fancy clothes, idle gossip, or cleverness will not last, "melting away like snow wreaths in the sun!"[4]

The Pair from Assisi

If we want to look at an example of virtue at work in the lives of true spiritual friends, then let's take a big step back to the Middle Ages and take a closer look at St. Francis and St. Clare of Assisi. The spiritual friends lifted up the Church of their time, advanced the cause of Franciscan spirituality, and left behind a legacy of love that continues to influence spiritual seekers of every Christian denomination to this day.

Francis and Clare are a friendship story for the ages. Their relationship was based on their mutual desire to love God before all else and to serve others in his name. Probably no other saintly "couple" is more famous than this dynamic medieval duo.

"Francis and Clare were magnetically drawn to each other by their powerful and passionate love of God, as their lives showed," wrote John Michael Talbot in his book *The Lessons of St. Francis.*[5]

Talbot and other experts on Francis and Clare constantly came back to the fact that the two hardly ever saw each other face to face in their lifetimes. They were together only a handful of times over the course of twenty years, and yet their relationship was stronger than anything most of us could ever hope to experience.

In his book *Light in the Dark Ages: The Friendship of Francis and Clare of Assisi,* author Jon M. Sweeney wrote: "Francis and Clare then became an unusual couple. The sources all indicate that they had a natural affection for one another. They were not married and they never had an affair, but their love for each other was felt palpably by those around them. . . . Their affection for and trust of each other fueled the early Franciscan movement and gave birth to a joy, beauty, and spirit that had long been absent from the faith."[6]

At the center of their relationship with each other and their lives in general was humility. Francis's spirituality of poverty and prayer, kindness and virtue is evident not only in the mission of the order he founded but also in his many writings, including his Prayer Before the Crucifix:

> Most high,
> glorious God,
> enlighten the darkness of my heart
> and give me, Lord,
> a correct faith,
> a certain hope,
> a perfect charity,

sense and knowledge,
so that I may carry out Your holy and
true command.[7]

Short, simple, and yet so direct. Faith, hope, and charity, the virtues that started this chapter, come back around again, over and over, as we explore not only spiritual friendship but also spiritual life in general. These are the intangible things that steer our spiritual friendships on right paths. They keep us from letting our God-driven relationships deteriorate into something mundane or banal.

We can look to Francis and Clare as models of virtue, not only in the individual lives they led but in the deep friendship they shared. You don't have to delve too deep below the surface of their writings and their work to see charity and kindness, honesty and patience. They nurtured these qualities first in their relationship with God, then in their friendship with one another, and finally in their commitment to their religious ideals in the greater world.

Their friendship, founded in their common love of God and their desire to put aside all worldly possessions in order to serve the poor and to be poor, did not require weekly visits or phone calls or face-to-face meetings. Their common purpose was enough to hold them together over time and distance. When they did meet, however, their connection and love for one another could not be denied.

In his book *The Sun and Moon Over Assisi: A Personal Encounter with Francis and Clare*, author Gerard Thomas Straub's description of the relationship between Francis and Clare sums up the kind of spiritual friendship we're exploring in this chapter and in this book:

> "No one captured the heart and spirit of Saint
> Francis's message more than Saint Clare, and
> no one ever came closer to following or reach-
> ing the Franciscan ideal than she. . . . If you
> want to know about Francis talk to Clare; she
> understood him better and loved him more
> than anyone else. She was, in short, his soul
> mate. And she died fighting to keep his dream
> alive."[8]

Spiritual friends know each other, love each other, understand each other in a very special way. Their connection
leads to great things—in their prayer lives, in their practical lives, in the things they do for their families, friends,
and community. Like Francis and Clare, spiritual friends
can inspire one another to spiritual greatness, all grounded
in humility, of course. They can coax each other along the
spiritual path, nudge each other to face a spiritual challenge
that may seem daunting, and shore each other up when one
or the other is struggling or maybe even veering off course.

Spiritual friendship, in short, starts with God, grows in
God, and ultimately finds its fulfillment in God.

Food for Thought

1. Think about your friendships. How do the virtues of
   humility, honesty, compassion, and charity play a role
   in practical ways in your current spiritual friendships?

2. Reflect on your friendship with God. How do you
   nurture that relationship? How does your relationship
   with God influence your spiritual friendships?

3. Friendships like the one between Francis de Sales
   and Jane de Chantal and between Francis and Clare

of Assisi prompted these friends to work for the good of others. Can you see how your own spiritual friendships might motivate you to serve others more fully?

Meditation

Our spiritual friendships are
a continual journey toward
what St. Paul called
the "bond of perfection,"
drawing us closer to God
and strengthening the virtues
of humility and patience,
charity and kindness.
We strive today and every day
to bear witness to those ideals,
even when it is a struggle.
We seek out those who
share our spiritual hunger
and build a community of love.
We base our lives on a friendship
first with God our Creator
and move ever outward
to encompass all in our reach.

Chapter 5

Communication:
Listening, Talking, and Praying Together

The greatest gift my friendship can give to you is the gift of your Belovedness. I can give that gift only insofar as I have claimed it for myself. Isn't that what friendship is all about: giving to each other the gift of our Belovedness?

—Henri J. M. Nouwen[1]

I n the months following the birth of my first child, Noah, in 1997, I went through the most serious crisis of faith I had ever experienced in my life. Before that time, I had felt twinges of occasional doubt or confusion here and there, but nothing compared to the experience of feeling betrayed by someone who had been a friend and a role model, someone in a position of power within the Church.

Considering the fact that my entire professional life was then—and continues to involve—writing for and about the Catholic Church, I could feel the repercussions of this particular faith crisis everywhere—at home, at work, and in the gaping void that now existed where my spiritual life had been. I was spiritually adrift and ill-equipped to find a way back to the heart of my faith life. I still believed deeply in God, still looked to Jesus as my savior, but at that point in my life, I could not get past the human weaknesses that had led me into this spiritual desert. Dennis, too, had been touched by this betrayal, and although he offered advice and comfort, he was too close to the situation to help me work my way out of it.

So I wrote to Ken, one of the few friends I was sure would not only listen, but would offer sage advice without judgment and spiritual counsel despite my protestations that I was done with church forever. I had met Ken twenty-five years earlier, when we were both working for *Catholic New York*, a weekly newspaper in Manhattan. I was a reporter, and Ken worked in production. We immediately forged a connection that went beyond eating lunch together in the cafeteria with our coworkers. We originally hit it off because of our shared love of music, a similar sense of humor, and an interest in the world around us, but we had something extra, too. We shared a spiritual hunger that led to deep discussions about everything from prayer to meditation to eucharist.

Ken was the one who introduced me to Thomas Merton's writing. And even now, he often recommends spiritual books or quotes or poems. In fact, my bookcase is full of books Ken has sent over the years to help guide my spiritual journey. He understood my interest in Eastern traditions like yoga and Zen and offered his own insights on how to incorporate them into my Catholic practices. Our conversations were "give and take," with both of us sharing some of our deepest spiritual longings.

When I moved from New York to Austin, Texas, Ken and I corresponded through regular and lengthy letters. We shared not only the basic news of the day but also delved into our ongoing spiritual struggles and discoveries, offering thoughts and insights, encouragement and prayers.

So when my crisis of faith hit, I knew that even though two thousand miles separated us, Ken would still be there for me, even if only in written correspondence. And he was. I have saved almost every letter Ken has sent me over the years, though e-mails have replaced those ten-page letters that were frequently handwritten. I still have both sides of our written conversation about my personal crisis tucked away in a file in my basement. Reading them recently brought it all back for a moment:

"For me this has gone from anger to disappointment to severe sadness to complete disconnectedness," I wrote to Ken in February 1998. "I have not been to church since August when this whole mess happened. . . . The lack of any spiritual life has left a huge void that has really affected me in negative ways. Even with this awareness, I can't go back. I even tried reading some Thomas Merton and other spiritual writings to try to jump-start my spiritual life. Nothing works. It makes me so sad."

In his compassionate yet faith-filled fashion, Ken responded to my cry for help. "Thank you for being so honest and sharing with me all that you're going through. How I feel for you! I have never been in a place like the place you're in now, and although I can't identify or share in what you're feeling, the fact that a close friend is aching in her heart—for whatever reason—makes my heart ache," he wrote, encouraging me to find a priest or nun who could sit down with me and talk about the spiritual and personal issues that were weighing so heavily on me. And even though he had never experienced such a faith crisis, he was able to relate my struggles to other types of struggles in his own life and share his wisdom and experience. Ken offered the most important thing one spiritual friend can do for another: he prayed for me.

"I will not just say a prayer for you. From this night forward, I will be lifting you up in every time of prayer, every day. I will offer your pain and doubt up to Jesus in every Communion I receive, in every Rosary I say for the healing of the world. I will pray for your healing every single day. All I ask in return is to open yourself, open your ears a little more, open your eyes a little more, open your heart a little more, and look, look, look for that slightest moment when the sun seems a bit brighter, a breeze a tiny bit more caressing, a look from your loved ones a little more special—that will be the Holy Spirit lifting you up. The Spirit passionately wants to fill you!"

Even now, more than ten years after that crisis, re-reading those letters touches my heart. I am reminded that I am blessed to have some very dear spiritual friends in my life. Although we no longer write long letters that arrive by mail with photos and news clippings and books enclosed, Ken and I still communicate by e-mail. We have not seen each other in years, and we rarely talk by phone. Ken is not a phone talker. But all that just goes to show that true friends, spiritual friends, can maintain a deep and lasting bond with sometimes imperfect communication methods, as long as that communication is heartfelt and honest and ongoing.

The Flow of Friendship

It just so happens that before I met my husband, Dennis, he, too, worked with Ken in the same Catholic newspaper office. They became close friends, too. When I returned to *Catholic New York* as managing editor in the early 1990s, the three of us were good friends. The deep friendship that began first between Ken and me and then later between Ken and Dennis eventually became a shared friendship among the three of us. In fact, once Dennis and I married and moved to Texas, our correspondence with Ken reflected this beautiful expansion, with every letter from him including some passages that were addressed specifically to Dennis, and others meant for me.

Our friendship with Ken was so strong that when Dennis and I had Noah, we knew that Ken was the one we wanted to be his godfather. When it came down to choosing someone who takes his faith seriously, we had no doubt that Ken was the obvious person for the job. We knew that he would be a true spiritual guide to Noah if something were to happen to us. The fact that we could know that without question did not come about because we went out for walks during lunch breaks or took the subway to the train station together. It came about because we listened closely to each other, wrote regularly to each other, prayed deeply for each other, and so were connected in a way that typical friends are not.

When I e-mailed Ken to tell him that I was writing about our spiritual friendship, he said that because we lived such distances from each other, our friendship has been strengthened by "a shared correspondence that has chronicled our own maturing in God."

I often tell Ken, who is about ten years my senior, that he is "far ahead of me" spiritually. He always argues that point, reminding me that a spiritual journey does not proceed in a straight line. Instead, it "curves toward the depths of the heart" so that we end up dealing again and again with things we thought were already resolved.

"I can see where I would appear to an outsider like a 'mentor' at times, but that implies a 'spiritual director/ directee' relationship, and all along, no matter how mentor-like I may have sounded, I'm sure you know and could always sense that my thoughts and words to you flowed from friendship and shared experience and a passionate love for God (that most often is rarely spoken) and never from a sense of superiority or being 'spiritually more experienced,'" Ken wrote to me by e-mail recently. "In a way, when I think back to all the times I poured things out to you, it was precisely because you were 'friend and spiritual companion' that I felt comfortable enough to let down my guard to share and confide such deep movements within me to you . . . but it's silly to justify these things. You are who you are, and I am who I am, and blessed be God."

Ken and I do not communicate with the same frequency that we once did. That's due to busy family and work lives. But we still "talk" by e-mail when one of us has something to share with the other. I will tell Ken about the current state of my spiritual life or various aspects of prayer life that I want to discuss. In return, I typically receive a long note that is so deep and so thoughtful that I often have to re-read it many times to let it all sink in. It may be "only" e-mail, but letters from Ken still have a way of opening my spiritual eyes or encouraging me when I am struggling. Because the early foundation of our spiritual friendship was built on our common spiritual quest for a deeper connection to God, our relationship has been able to withstand the distance and time and decrease in communication that might have leveled another friendship. I know that all I have to do is pick up the phone or send an e-mail or letter, and the friendship that has figured so prominently in my past will once again be powerfully present.

Laying the Foundation of Communication

Before we get to a point in a friendship where we might pour out our hearts on a page or computer screen, we need to build a relationship based on trust and honesty and a willingness to share openly and from the heart. There are several key things that serve as the foundation of all other communication: listening, talking, and praying. Obviously, listening and talking are typical things that would be part of *any* friendship, not just spiritual friendships. But we're not talking about idle conversations, or work conversations, or conversations about parenting or sports, or other everyday topics. We're talking about taking conversation basics to a much deeper level.

Listening and talking between spiritual friends must occur in a place of trust. That trust will build up slowly, over time, as friends get to know one another better and share first a little about their interior lives. And, of course, that trust is built up as you also enjoy your friendship in more typical ways. Spiritual friendship is not only about praying and talking about God. That's at the heart of it, but it's by no means all of it. My friendship with Ken, for example, included lots of laughs, talking about everything from baseball to folk music to parenting. We're not just friends who talk about spiritual topics. We have a well-rounded friendship and know how to laugh and pray together.

To build a relationship of trust, friends must know they are safe to say what they need to say. They must know that their confidences will be kept, and that they will not be judged harshly or ridiculed. We all have friends with whom we're happy to share *part* of our lives but perhaps not *all* of our lives. We know we need to protect ourselves by keeping certain aspects of our interior lives private. That's not so with spiritual friendships. In spiritual friendship we must be able to talk about matters of the heart and spirit without fear or self-consciousness. In return, we must be willing to listen to our spiritual friends in the same spirit of openness and compassion.

This idea of trust and openness in friendship is described eloquently in one of the many letters between Thomas Merton and Catherine de Hueck Doherty, founder of Madonna House, a Catholic community of men and women dedicated to preaching the gospel through lives of service and prayer.

"For nothing is more sacred than a letter or a conversation in which one human being opens his or her heart to another, who factually has no right (like a priest in confession) to that confidence," Doherty wrote on October 25, 1941. "So it becomes at once both a tremendous privilege and a heavy, God-given responsibility."[2]

Doherty and Merton shared a spiritual friendship that began in 1941, before Merton had even decided to enter the Trappists. Over the years, until their last correspondence in 1966, they sent letters back and forth, talking about their callings, their latest projects, their writing efforts, their spiritual journeys, and their need for prayers.

In July 1963, when Doherty wrote to Merton, she touched on the reality that even the closest spiritual friends often cannot stay in constant communication. Yet, as I have experienced in my own friendship with Ken, the separation does not diminish the bond.

"It is always thus with us, you and me. You had written me November 12, 1962, and I am answering you on July 29, 1963. . . . Yet I know I do not have to apologize for the delay, because there really hasn't been a delay. You know I have answered your letter many times over, and that we have met; and in a manner of speaking, 'discussed it' in many strange places, in many quiet places, where people who both try to love God and one another the way God wants them to, meet!"[3]

In other words, spiritual friends are always connected, always in a kind of mental and spiritual communication, even when they are not talking or writing. In a sense, they feel as if they are together, as Doherty explains so beautifully, even when they are not. This kind of deep bond is not something that develops overnight, but grows slowly as trust builds. That kind of communion between friends can develop only with open communication that truly allows friends to enter into each other's hearts.

Old-Fashioned Communication in a New-Fangled World

When it comes to communication, the twenty-first-century man and woman should not be at a loss for words. We can "talk" to each other not only the old-fashioned way—in person or by telephone—but by e-mail, cell phone, instant message, texting, and handheld electronic "assistants." If anything, our communication with family members, friends, and even spiritual friends should be better than ever. And yet, it's not.

It's not for lack of interest. In fact, people are hungry for deeper, lasting friendships in this world where so much is temporary. Unfortunately, our American lifestyle simply doesn't lend itself to the time and commitment it takes to build such friendships. We have more demands on our schedules and less leisure time than ever. Our jobs take us to new cities and new neighborhoods. Many live side by side with neighbors who remain complete strangers. It has become harder to build community.

And while all the amazing instantaneous methods of communication at our disposal allow us to communicate quickly and frequently, they don't necessarily lend themselves to communicating deeply and spiritually. It's hard to take time away from all of our many responsibilities to write a "real" letter (even one sent by e-mail) if we can "tweet" someone in 140 characters or less.

Letter writing was once an art form, whether we're talking about letters from just a few decades ago or from many centuries ago. Letters take time, thought, and a certain seriousness even when they contain humor and funny anecdotes. Those qualities simply don't adapt that well to today's forms of rapid-fire communication. Add to that the fact that e-mail and texting are fleeting. They can't be gathered together and tied up with a ribbon to be taken out and savored at a later date. Today there's an emphasis on communication quantity but not necessarily on communication quality.

When it comes to spiritual friendship, quality counts. Obviously, spiritual friends are not those people on the other end of mass e-mails that we might forward. Spiritual friends are those people who inspire you to sit down and write something or say something "real," something that touches your heart or something that might touch your friend's heart. Communication is key when it comes to spiritual friendship.

St. Francis de Sales, in *Introduction to the Devout Life*, talked about communication in spiritual friendship as critical to its existence and growth, saying that "real" friendships are the "most dangerous of all affections" because unlike other relationships, friendship cannot exist without "mental communication."[4]

How could a real friendship be dangerous? St. Francis meant that because real friendship requires a deep sharing of personal feelings and emotions, it can be riskier than other relationships—even romantic love. Love can be unrequited, or love can exist without deep mental communication. But true friendship, he explained, is founded on a willingness to share the most intimate thoughts about God and spiritual life. It is about being vulnerable before another because you trust that this beloved friend will not reveal the confidences you share. This is a person who will not laugh or judge you harshly, will not turn away from you. Friendship must always be a two-way street that involves both friends contributing to the relationship and both friends loving each other in a mutual and respectful way.

When Francis talked about danger in such a relationship, he was also reminding us that opening ourselves up to another in such a way can take the friendship in a direction it should not go. We might be moving from a mutual but platonic love to something less pure. So spiritual friendship is at once deep, intimate, and vulnerable, but unless the friend is also a spouse, it should not cross the line to romantic love.

"All love is not friendship, for one may love without any return, and friendship implies mutual love. Further, those who are bound by such affection must be conscious that it is reciprocal—otherwise there may be love but not friendship—and moreover, there must be something communicated between the friends as a solid foundation of friendship," St. Francis de Sales wrote.[5]

Later on, in a chapter titled "Further Advice Concerning Intimacies," St. Francis de Sales remarked, "Friendship demands very close correspondence between those who love one another, otherwise it can never take root or continue. And together with the interchange of friendship, other things imperceptibly glide in, and a mutual giving and receiving of emotions and inclinations takes place. . . ."[6]

St. Francis de Sales practiced what he preached when it came to communicating with his friends. His letters, not only to his closest spiritual friend, St. Jane de Chantal, but to many others who came to him for spiritual direction, displayed the care and seriousness with which he approached those in his circle of spiritual friends.

In the preface to *Francis de Sales, Jane de Chantal: Letters of Spiritual Direction*, renowned theologian Henri J. M. Nouwen talked about how their seventeenth-century letters were still relevant to those of us seeking to strengthen spiritual friendships today. He pondered how modern friends can forge the kind of relationship that existed between Francis and Jane.

"In our distrustful, fearful, fragmented world constantly exploding in violence and destruction, friendships such as lived out by Francis and Jane and expressed in these letters point the way to healing, reconciliation and new life," Nouwen wrote. "How to develop and nurture such friendships? This book suggests that writing letters may still be one of the most fruitful ways."[7]

Instead of watching TV, Nouwen suggested, we could write letters to those we consider spiritual friends. Not e-mails dashed off without so much as a spell check and not letters about the minutia of our days, but old-fashioned personal letters. Our letters to our spiritual friends should focus on our spiritual joys and struggles and encourage our friends to share their feelings and spiritual thoughts as well. Whether we do that with a paper and pen or at a computer screen is really a matter of an individual choice. Either one is fine. In fact, technology can work to our advantage, if we use it with care.

"During the quiet, peaceful hours that we spend communicating God's love to others in our letters, we build a

new community and bring light into the world. This is what
Francis and Jane did in their time. This is what we still can
do in ours. I have little doubt that the fruits will be plenti-
ful," Nouwen wrote.[8]

It's unfortunate that letter writing has fallen out of favor, but it's not impossible to bring at least a little of that lost
art back into our friendships and our lives. We don't have to
sit down and handwrite ten pages on fancy stationery. Even
e-mail can be a means of deep and meaningful communication, if it's done right. We simply need to remember that no
matter how hectic our schedules or how rusty our letter-
writing skills, we have to take some time on a regular basis
to communicate with spiritual friends in ways that deepen
our relationships and further our journey toward God.

Prayer as Communication

A wonderful letter from St. Francis de Sales to St. Jane de
Chantal, dated February 11, 1607, gives a real sense of just
how critical communication was to their friendship: "I was
ten whole weeks without a word from you, my dear, my
very dear daughter, and your last letters were written early
last November. But one good thing is that my patience had
almost given out and I think it would have given out entirely if I hadn't remembered that I must preserve it in order to
be free to preach it to others. But at last, my dearest daughter, yesterday a bundle arrived, like a fleet from India, full
of letters and spiritual songs. Oh, how welcome it was and
how I loved it!"[9]

St. Francis's letters to St. Jane cover substantial spiritual
ground. He discussed with her prayer and contemplation,

virtue, Christian friendship, the reception of Communion, and much more. Always in the background, however, was their fiercely strong friendship, which allowed them to "talk" with such openness and freedom.

Spiritual friendships rely not only on communication, but also on a deep and constant connection to God. These are not letters or e-mails or conversations about frivolous pursuits, although it's fine if your communication includes that, too. These are communications that address the things that are often kept hidden in the recesses of our hearts. These are things that we are often afraid to bring into the light of day because our "regular" friends would think we were "holy" or weird. And that leads us to the other critical component of spiritual friendship: prayer.

Prayer is a topic that we will come back to again and again in this book because it is a centerpiece of spiritual friendships. Prayer can bind us to our spiritual friends even when we can't see them for long stretches. We may pray with one another or for one another. Our prayers may take the form of words spoken together, either as part of a small faith community or in a prayer group or standing side by side at Mass. Our prayers may take the form of meditations or reflections on our mutual spiritual journeys. Or our prayers may take the form of shared silence. These could be moments when we put aside listening and talking to simply sit together in the beauty of the most sacred of all sounds—God's silence.

Catherine de Hueck Doherty also founded the Friendship House network to serve the poor. In August 1956, in a letter to Thomas Merton, she wrote, "I know you are praying for us, and I know that you know that I am praying for you always."[10] She comments that their mutual prayers are more powerful than anything she could write in a letter.

And in January 1958, she wrote: "You are in my humble poor little prayers daily. Strange as it might seem, you are closer to me as time goes by than you ever were in FH [Friendship House]."[11]

Prayer keeps spiritual friends linked on their journeys in a way that surpasses anything that can be said with words or put on paper. Often it is only with our spiritual friends that we are comfortable even talking about prayer and about our reliance on God. Spiritual friendship without prayer is like a ship without a rudder. We may move, but we probably won't reach our destination.

Modern Methods

Don't worry. Not all of us are going to wax poetic in long letters to spiritual friends. We need to accept our own comfort zones and time constraints. We should do whatever works for us. Prayerful communication between spiritual friends can be as simple as a scripture quote or a line from a spiritual text e-mailed to lift a person up in the middle of a busy work week. In those cases, e-mail and texting can be a true blessing for spiritual friends. They can provide a way to insert a spiritual connection into an ordinary day.

We can learn to use technology to our advantage, relying on letter writing and serious conversation as the mainstay of our spiritual friendships, but using the best our high-tech world has to offer to stay spiritually in touch, even when we are far apart and otherwise occupied.

Pope Benedict XVI recognized the importance of using technology for spiritual purposes when he released his message for the forty-third World Communications Day in 2009. He talked about the "extraordinary potential" of digital technologies to connect people and create opportunities for dialogue and friendship.

"The desire for connectedness and the instinct for communication that are so obvious in contemporary culture are best understood as modern manifestations of the basic and enduring propensity of humans to reach beyond themselves and to seek communion with others. In reality, when we open ourselves to others, we are fulfilling our deepest need and becoming more fully human," he wrote. "Loving is, in fact, what we are designed for by our Creator. Naturally, I am not talking about fleeting, shallow relationships, I am talking about the real love that is at the very heart of Jesus' moral teaching."[12]

Today, we have immediate access to friends and family and colleagues through social networks like Facebook and Twitter. Not only can we talk to them "live" online, but we can monitor everything they're doing through status updates and photos posted on their pages. We know when friends are on vacation, when a brother is at home sick, when nieces and nephews have won awards at school, when friends are changing jobs. And while that does allow us to stay in more constant contact, we have to be careful, as the pope points out in his message. We should not allow the superficial side of social networking to replace deep relationships that require care and time.

Of course, the positive side of social networking is that it may allow us to stay connected to—or reconnect with—a community of friends we would otherwise lose touch with. I was leery of Facebook when I first signed up, but within a week I was corresponding with people I hadn't talked to in twenty-five years. Many Facebook friendships haven't moved beyond polite conversation about kids and work and vacation. A few others, however, have developed into interesting online friendships. A woman who went to high school with me is now the wife of a Lutheran minister. The two of us have connected in a way we never did as teenagers. Two other Facebook friendships have even sparked a request to start a spiritual reading group here in my hometown. None of that would have happened without the use of social networking. But because of my posts, which often include spiritual references or writings, others with similar interests have sought me out, and new connections have been forged.

Although we do need to watch for the dangers of relying too heavily on high-tech communication when building spiritual friendships, we also need to be careful not to shut the door on it out of fear or distrust. This new way of creating community from a distance has the potential to reconnect us with friends who may turn out to share our spiritual hunger.

Social networking can also open the door to bringing friends together in prayer. A quick look at my homepage and I can quickly find a friend asking for prayers because her mother was just diagnosed with breast cancer. Another friend is asking for prayers as she goes on a job interview.

In some ways, there are many benefits to be mined from the digital communication age, if we do as Pope Benedict has suggested. We must make sure that our dialogue is "rooted in a genuine and mutual searching for truth."[13]

By combining what is available to us through modern means of communication with more traditional and critical elements—like listening, talking, writing, and praying—spiritual friends can nourish the bond between them and lay the foundation for a lifelong relationship that can stand the test of time and distance.

Food for Thought

1. Think about those friendships where you feel safe and experience real trust. How do you build trust in your relationships? What do you need to feel comfortable enough to open up and share from the heart?

2. Reflect on your current friendships, and choose one that might lead to deeper levels of communication. How might you make a stronger connection? What communication methods best suit your personality?

3. Prayer plays a significant role in keeping spiritual friends linked even when they live far apart. How can you build deeper prayer connections into your friendships? Are there any specific spiritual practices that would lend themselves to nurturing your friendships?

Meditation

The seeds of spiritual friendship
must be nurtured and tended
if they are to grow and blossom
into something transforming.
Today, we pray for the grace
to recognize these friendships
in their earliest stages,
to take the time
to nudge them along through
ongoing spiritual conversations,
written affirmations, and shared prayers.
These friendships are gifts from God,
proof of the Spirit at work in our lives.
We honor them and celebrate them today.

Chapter 6

Kindred Spirits:
Friendships Come in All Forms

A friend loves at all times, and is born, as is a brother, for adversity.
—Proverbs 17:17

For me, there is no question that my first spiritual friend was my mother. Although we shared a close parent-child bond, we also shared something that went far beyond that. We shared a deep love of the Church, something that my mother had instilled in me throughout my life. That shared passion drew us together in unexpected ways and allowed us to sidestep a lot of the typical tensions that often exist between parents and maturing children. We still argued occasionally over the usual teenage issues— curfews and dating and clothes. But as I began to move from childhood into adulthood, our relationship flowed easily toward friendship. True friendship.

Our lives were intertwined not just at home but at our local parish. We both taught fourth-grade religion. I ran the Catholic Youth Organization, and my mother served as an advisor. She was a constant chaperone, something I loved rather than loathed as many teens might. My mother's devotion to her faith and the Church was instrumental in my eventually choosing a career as a Catholic journalist, which she enjoyed vicariously for a few years before she died at the age of forty-seven.

Our friendship was not without its rocky stretches. We discussed everything and often disagreed. But even our disagreements were conducted not in an angry sort of way, but in the way that good friends go back and forth on various topics in order to move deeper into them and to sort out the good from the bad. Through her example and her willingness to accept me not only as daughter but also as friend, my mother taught me what it really means to love someone unconditionally. She managed to pack a lot into the all-too-brief twenty-five years we had together. I often wonder how the special bond we shared would have developed had we been given an opportunity to build on our early spiritual friendship as I grew into my roles as a wife, mother, writer, and spiritual seeker.

My relationship with my mother is a true-life example of spiritual friendships within families. You may wonder how a parent or sibling or even a cousin can really be a spiritual friend. If we're related, aren't we already connected in a deep enough way—for life? Although that's true, certain relatives, just like certain neighbors or co-workers, may connect with us in special ways. We may have the same interests or hobbies. We may find it easy to talk to each other. And, in the case of spiritual friendship, we may share a passion for God and a hunger to move forward on our spiritual journey side by side.

That certainly was the case with my mother. We loved many of the same things. My mom had a beautiful singing voice and was a born performer. I inherited her love of music and sang in a band for many years. She was a gifted cook and baker. I picked up enough of her skills to hold my own in the kitchen. We loved similar clothes and movies, similar books and music. Despite our twenty-two-year age difference, people often thought we were sisters. And all of those things are nice and, in many ways, normal. But what took our relationship from a parent-and-child relationship to a spiritual friendship was our mutual hunger for a deeper spiritual life. We connected on a different level, a place where God took precedence over the more typical roles we filled and allowed us to become something more.

My interest in spiritual things came directly from my mother. She taught me about a loving God. She showed me how to pray and then prayed at my side, not only when I was a little child being tucked into bed, but when I was a young adult kneeling next to her at Mass. She demonstrated to me an absolute trust in God's plan, even when his plan included suffering and loss and heartache. That doesn't mean that I didn't question that plan during difficult times. But because of the bond I shared with my mother, any doubt or confusion always came back around full circle until I was standing once again in front of God, waiting expectantly for whatever was next.

When my mother was diagnosed with cancer in 1987 at the age of forty-seven, I was preparing to move across the country. I had quit my job at *Catholic New York* newspaper and packed my car. Then we got the news that the colon cancer that seemed so curable at first was far worse than what her doctors expected. I changed my plans and stayed in New York, driving my mother to doctor appointments and sitting with her at home while she recovered from the ravages of chemotherapy. In the last nine months of her life, we not only had time to talk, but also to pray. Together, we were able to acknowledge that the future was probably not going to turn out as we had hoped.

On a Saturday morning in April 1988, my mother took a turn for the worse. The chemo and the cancer had become more than she could bear. Her once strong body had betrayed her. She couldn't even sip a cup of coffee. I remember sitting on her bed, watching her rest and admitting to myself, perhaps for the first time, that she was dying slowly before my eyes. She must have sensed me watching because she woke up and watched me cry. The message was clear, even without words; we both knew that this was the end.

I reached out to hug her and realized how frail her body had become. It felt as though she would snap in two. That was the last time I hugged my mother when she was still able to hug me back. As I rocked with her on her bed, my tears dropping onto her face, I asked her not to leave me, to stay and be part of my future. What she said in reply was, "All I wanted was a little girl." (I was her firstborn.) It was the last time we talked privately, the last time she told me she loved me.

Over the next few days, she deteriorated rapidly, until early in the morning of April 12. When she awoke from a coma, the whole family was sleeping on the floor around her bed in our family room. She opened her eyes and cried. She was more alert than she had been since that Saturday when I had sat with her in her room. She looked at each of us as tears rolled down her face. It was clear to us that she was letting us know that she knew we were with her until the end. As she struggled to breathe, we laid our heads on her bed, her hands, her head just to be close to her. We told her that it was okay for her to go.

I was holding her hand when she took her last breath. One minute she was there and the next she was gone. I lost a mother and a dear friend that day. When it came time to plan her funeral Mass, I knew what she wanted. It wasn't because she had specified it, but because I knew her spirit so well that there was simply no question in my mind about what readings and music to select. We were connected on a soul-to-soul level, as spiritual friends often are.

Although I am also close with my father and my siblings, the bond I shared with my mother was unique. I was blessed to have been her daughter, her friend, her confidant, and her spiritual companion.

All in the Family

Many of us can probably think of people in our families—immediate and extended—who are natural "candidates" for spiritual friends. They are the family members with whom we tend to discuss our faith, the people who bring out our spiritual side, the ones who have strong faith lives of their own and are eager to share what they've learned and experienced. And, to top it off, we probably enjoy an easy camaraderie with them, talking and sharing without any self-consciousness.

Unfortunately, we don't always have the opportunities these days to spend extended periods of time with family members who may live across the country. So discovering that diamond in the rough—the spiritual friend in the making—within our own families can be trickier today than it once was.

We don't have to look too far back into our nation's history to find a time when family life was very different than it is today. I'm not just talking about the way immediate families are pulled in a million different directions, driving children to countless extracurricular activities while juggling work and volunteer schedules. Many American households today have to operate more like small corporations than small faith communities. I'm talking about extended families that are so often separated by thousands of miles. Parents and children, grandchildren and siblings, aunts and uncles, nieces, nephews, and cousins are deprived of the kind of overarching support network that many of us took for granted growing up.

In her book *The Friendship Crisis: Finding, Making, and Keeping Friends When You're Not a Kid Anymore*, Marla Paul talks about the problems that often go hand-in-hand with our very mobile society. In a chapter called "Ripping Up Your Roots and Sinking New Ones," she focuses on the "emotional wrench" of having to rebuild lives and friendships in new communities every few years.

"When we're unplugged from friends, we may devolve from our once confident selves and begin to question our likeability. My self-assurance plummeted after I moved to Dallas. When I prepared to entertain my new next-door neighbor, my hands were as icy as if I were going on the blind date. The stakes seemed so high. . . . Even though a bevy of devoted pals may live several states away, the transition between leaving old relationships and bridging new ones can knock us off balance."[1]

Unfortunately, that feeling of being rootless is all too common for Americans today. Leaving our hometowns and extended families behind is a way of life. Back in the "good old days," we didn't have far to go to find someone to talk to, someone to help us through a tough time, someone to celebrate with us or cry with us or laugh with us. Families lived blocks away, not states away, and they tended to circle first around one another and then around their local church. We had a built-in connection to faith and to what it means to live our faith out in the world through our ancestors, who weren't some far-off, unknown ideal but real, living, breathing relatives right in our own backyards.

In earlier generations, people kept each other honest, so to speak. The mere presence of a large extended family infused its members with a certain accountability—to themselves and to the rest of the clan. It was all for one, and one for all. Consequently, these families often laid the foundation for the kinds of relationships that could develop into spiritual friendships later on. That's not to say that days gone by produced more spiritual friendships. But the close proximity to lots of cousins and aunts and uncles certainly increased the chances that a relative might, in fact, turn out to be a spiritual friend as well.

Relatives as Friends: Role Models to Follow

We can look back into our Church history and discover deep spiritual friendships between those who not only shared a home and relatives, but also a spiritual hunger and values. Look at the lives of some of the great saints and you'll find that many of them shared spiritual friendships with parents and siblings, even when it wasn't easy. Think of St. Monica, who refused to give up on her son, Augustine. Think of Benedict and Scholastica, siblings who rarely saw each other and yet shared a deep commitment to monastic life. Think of St. Thérèse of Lisieux, the "Little Flower" whose sisters, Marie and Pauline, were in the convent with her. It was the Little Flower's sisters who encouraged her to write what would become her famous and best-selling autobiography, *Story of a Soul*.

We don't know much about Benedict and Scholastica of Nursia other than what was written by Pope St. Gregory the Great in the seventh century. In his *Dialogues*, Pope St. Gregory said that these sibling saints may have been twins. They saw each other only once a year when they met for prayer and spiritual discussions. And yet, they were deeply connected to one another. Scholastica was the first Benedictine nun, who lived in a convent near her brother's monastery at Monte Cassino.

Legend has it that the siblings were gathered for their annual spiritual meeting when Scholastica asked Benedict and his monks to remain there through the night so that they could continue their spiritual discussion. But Benedict refused and didn't want to stay outside his abbey. Even though they were brother and sister, Scholastica was not allowed to enter Benedict's monastery. So, they had to meet elsewhere for their annual talks.

St. Gregory the Great told their story in chapter 33 of *Dialogues*:

"The sky was so clear at the time that there was not a cloud in sight. At her brother's refusal Scholastica folded her hands on the table and rested her head upon them in earnest prayer. When she looked up again, there was a sudden burst of lightning and thunder, accompanied by such a downpour that Benedict and his companions were unable to set a foot outside the door."[2]

Scholastica cried as she prayed, and Benedict, on seeing that he could not return to his abbey because of the storm, asked that God forgive Scholastica for what she had wrought through her prayers.

"He had no choice now but to stay, in spite of his unwillingness. They spent the entire night together and both of them derived great profit from the holy thoughts they exchanged about the interior life."[3]

Scholastica, who was founder and abbess of the Benedictine sisters, died only three days after this meeting. Benedict had her body brought to his monastery, where it was put in the tomb he had set aside for himself. When he died in 547, he was buried with her.

These were siblings who impacted each other in very big ways. St. Benedict, whose Rule continues to guide monastic communities around the world, no doubt reaped spiritual benefits from his close friendship with his sister. The two were clearly connected to each other in a spiritual companionship that went far beyond familial ties. Through their shared loved of God and their willingness to turn to each other for support and guidance on their spiritual journeys, they not only directed their own lives toward heaven but influenced religious life in the Western world for all time.

We know a lot more about St. Thérèse of Lisieux and her sisters thanks to the saint's autobiography. This spiritual classic details her relationship with members of her family and their influence on her spiritual life. Thérèse was born in 1873, the youngest of nine children. Her mother died when she was only four years old. She considered her sister Pauline her second mother. Later, Pauline was prioress of the Carmelite monastery where all three sisters took their vows and lived. Thérèse then considered Pauline as her mother in two ways—familial and spiritual. It was her sister Marie who suggested to Thérèse that she write the story of her life. Pauline ensured that the book was completed before this saint's death at age twenty-four.

It is obvious that these three sisters enjoyed a spiritual friendship that moved beyond the bounds of their family love. They had other siblings, yet these three shared a passion for their faith that bound them together in a powerful and unusual way.

In her *Story of a Soul*, Thérèse recalled sitting on Marie's knee, taking in all she told her about God and prayer. "I think that all the warmth and greatness of her soul entered mine. . . . She showed me how one could achieve sanctity by being faithful in the smallest matters."[4]

Later, Thérèse reflected on her First Communion and the day Pauline was received into Carmel: "There I saw you, Pauline, become the bride of Jesus, with your veil, white like mine, and your crown of roses. There was no trace of sadness in my joy, for I hoped to join you soon and wait for heaven at your side."[5]

We find a modern-day version of this kind of sibling spiritual friendship between Pope Benedict XVI and his brother, Georg Ratzinger. George and Joseph were both altar boys back in Aschau, Bavaria, attended the seminary in Traunstein and Freising, were ordained on the same day in 1951, and celebrated their first Mass together.

The brothers remained spiritually close throughout their lives, encouraging and advising each other in their respective positions in the Church. After Joseph Ratzinger became Pope Benedict in 2005, the two talked on the phone frequently. Georg—Msgr. Ratzinger—was often seen in the role of protector, defending his younger brother in the press against criticisms over various issues. He visited his brother, the pope, for weeks at a time at the pope's summer residence in Castel Gandolfo.

"From the beginning of my life my brother has always been for me not only a companion, but also a trustworthy guide. For me he has been a point of orientation and of reference with the clarity and determination of his decisions. He has always shown me the path to take, even in difficult situations," the pope wrote in August 2008, when he made his brother an honorary citizen of Castel Gandolfo.[6] Reflecting back on their boyhood years in Regensburg, the pope continued: "My brother has pointed out that since then, we have arrived at the last stage of our lives, at old age. The days left to live progressively diminish. But also in this stage my brother helps me to accept with serenity, with humility and with courage the weight of each day. I thank him."[7]

We don't have to exhibit the intensity or shared vocations that are seen in the lives of Sts. Benedict and Scholastica, in the lives of Thérèse and her sisters, or even in the lives of Pope Benedict XVI and his brother. In many different ways, we can experience spiritual friendship within our families. These unique friendships exist in all times and in all places. But just as we look to the recorded lives of the saints for general spiritual guidance, so too we can look to saintly or at least publicly known spiritual friends to lead us down a similar path. We simply need to open our eyes, ears, and hearts to the possibility that a sibling or parent or cousin may be someone we can connect with on a deeper level. This family member could be someone who can be a true spiritual companion for the rest of our lives.

Friendship within Marriage

One of the most obvious spiritual friendships within families is that which can grow between spouses. In Christian marriages, spiritual friendship should be a natural by-product. It can and should emerge from the kind of love and devotion that husbands and wives declare when they commit themselves to each other in the sacrament of matrimony.

St. Francis de Sales addressed the role of spiritual friendship within marriage in *Introduction to the Devout Life* when he wrote, "Mere sensual intercourse is not worthy of the name friendship; and were there nothing more in married love it would not deserve to bear the name; but inasmuch as that involves the participation of life, industry, possessions, affections and an unalterable fidelity, marriage, when rightly understood, is a very real and holy friendship."[8]

My husband, Dennis, has often teased me about the fact that I tend to relate more to spiritual realities than he does. In fact, however, our relationship started out first as a friendship with built-in spiritual values. We were both working for *Catholic New York* newspaper in Manhattan when we became friends. We were drawn together as friends by our common interests, common friends, and similarities in our sense of humor. We share a "New York sense of humor," that is, a sense of humor peppered with lots of sarcasm and rapid-fire comebacks that can make other people's heads spin if they're not used to it. We have one friend who says he has to make sure he's really on his game if he's going to keep up with our back-and-forth comments and jokes when he visits.

Of course, a sense of humor is just one part of what my friendship with Dennis is all about. We are also both writers, Catholic writers, who love to talk about current events, culture, politics, and, obviously, the Church. We are both Italian and Irish. We both love good food, especially Italian food, and spending time at home rather than running from one thing to another. Dennis is more of a quiet introvert, while I am a talkative extrovert. So, we complement each other's personalities as well.

In our early days, after we began dating and went from being office friends to an engaged couple, our relationship sparked a shared desire for a spiritual renewal. Both of us had been "away" from the Church in a certain sense even though we worked for the Church. We were focused more on the business of the Church rather than on the heart of our faith. But together, inspired by our conversations about faith and about what we were looking for in life, we found that we wanted to recapture the essence of spiritual life. We wanted to not only make our individual lives better, but also make our lives as a couple better as well.

We began praying together in the evenings using a devotional Bible for couples, given to us by a priest who worked on the same floor we did in the New York Catholic Center. We attended Mass together on Sundays at Our Lady of the Assumption Church in the Bronx. I began attending daily Mass, something I hadn't done in years. It was as if our friendship-turned-courtship brought with it a spiritual rebirth that we had been searching for without even realizing it. It was, as mentioned in an earlier chapter, one of those moments where two people find each other and realize that they were never really alone after all.

When we decided to get married, we spent more time planning the liturgy than we did planning the reception. Faith had become our focus. Sure, we still wanted to have great Italian food, but more importantly, we wanted the readings and songs to reflect what we had rediscovered together. We wanted every detail to speak of the joy we felt not only in having found each other, but also in having found a renewed faith life. At the time of our wedding, the pastor who married us was also our friend. We felt as if God had brought him into our lives at a time when we needed someone to help us move forward to this new place in our spiritual journey.

When we walked down the aisle on April 29, 1995, surrounded by family and friends, it was clear to both of us that our vows were not just about staying together and raising a family, but about growing together spiritually and making our home and our lives a place where God came first.

With three children in our lives now, a lot has changed since those early days. We spend so much of our time trying to stay one step ahead of our many responsibilities that it's easy to lose sight of where we started. But the foundation that we built at the very beginning of our relationship is the very thing that sustains us and keeps us stable as we face the tumultuous twists and turns of contemporary family life. We still stand side by side at Mass each week, even if we do so while wrangling with our four-year-old. We still say grace before meals each night, even if half the family is already chewing when we start. We still make a point of marking the seasons of our Church year—Advent and Christmas, Lent and Easter—with special rituals, prayers, and celebrations. We both still work for the Church, me as a writer and Dennis as director of Communications for the New York State Catholic Conference. And so our daily lives still include ongoing conversations throughout the day—at the breakfast table, by e-mail, by instant message—about the faith and the Church.

Those are the things that keep my spiritual friendship with Dennis strong even when it sometimes feels to us as if it's been parked in neutral for a few years. I think it's important for married couples to remember that their spiritual friendships will go through ups and downs, and periods of intensity and tepidness. If we recognize the steady presence of that friendship in the background, we can shift our attitudes and move forward even when we think there's no time for it.

In his book *For Better . . . Forever! A Catholic Guide to Lifelong Marriage*, author and psychologist Gregory Popcak says that marriage has the "power to transform prayer life."[9] But that shouldn't be understood in the usual or traditional sense.

"Saints are transparent. Their love and service always leads their admirers to God, who shines through them. Be a saint to your spouse and children. Let the Lord shine though the loving, generous service you give—joyfully—every day. Pray your marriage, and let God's grace transform you and your loved ones through that living prayer," Popcak wrote.[10]

What does it mean to "pray your marriage"? How can we become a "living prayer" that will transform others? Popcak explained that we may have to update our definition of prayer. He said that he once thought of prayer as something he *did*—attending eucharistic adoration, saying the rosary, and so forth. When work and family commitments began to make it difficult for him to find blocks of time for traditional prayer, he started to see prayer in a new light, as something he could *be* rather than something he should do.

"I am beginning to understand how to use my life and marriage as a prayer; how to find God, and spiritual growth, in the 'little things,' the daily activities, sacrifices, and challenges that are part and parcel of my vocation of husband and father," he writes, adding that working each day to become a better husband and father is "the best spiritual exercise" he can do.[11]

"Whether you realize it or not, everything you do in the context of your sacramental marriage—from your work and other roles, to the little pecks on the cheek you give each other, to your getting off the couch when you're tired in order to play with or serve your family, to the arguments you have, to your lovemaking—is prayer," Popcak wrote.[12]

His book may not be about spiritual friendship per se, but what Popcak described is exactly what is needed to feed spiritual friendships within a family. We will not develop deep spiritual bonds with those closest to us if we do not take on the role of a servant. That doesn't mean that we run around picking up after everyone without expecting them to contribute to the family. It means that when we need to do something for someone, we should do it with the heart of Jesus. And on those occasions when we may have to pick up the slack for someone else or overlook a habit that tends to annoy us, we do it not to lord it over another, but to quietly serve as Jesus would serve.

Of course, that's not always an easy row to hoe. We can get worn out by the responsibilities of daily life. But joyful and loving service is the way to plant the seeds of Christian love within our families. That love will blossom into the kinds of real friendship that take us beyond the basic relationships of husband and wife, parent and child, brother and sister.

Like Siblings, but Not

In the realm of spiritual friendships, there are certain relationships that are like the bonds between spiritual sibling friends and yet exist between unrelated people. Typically these friendships form between men or between women whose lives intersect at some point. Friendships emerge where people have a common goal, a shared set of values, a similar approach to spirituality and faith, and a commitment to walking that path together.

In his book *Running to the Mountain: A Journey of Faith and Change*, author Jon Katz talks about his close friendship with Jeff, another writer. Jeff, the author says, was like a father, but also like a peer, a brother, and a friend. Nearing the age of fifty, Katz decided to buy a ramshackle house in the mountains of upstate New York. The house was discovered by Jeff who lived in a nearby town because Jeff often traveled to the mountains to enjoy the view and spend time in solitude.

Not a man fond of formal religion, Katz set off on his spiritual journey with his two dogs and a pile of Thomas Merton books. His wife and daughter offered their support and encouragement from their New Jersey home. Katz spent months at a time letting the silence of the mountain and the words of Merton lead him to a place of truth. And through it all—through life changes and financial struggles, work issues and family obligations—his friendship with Jeff remained a critical part of his journey to spiritual discovery.

"If traumas tend to open us up, friends help keep us that way, showing and teaching, coaxing us out of our own experiences, giving us the strength to take a chance and helping us heal when we fall on our heads. With them, we can relax, feel safe, talk openly," Katz wrote. "A spiritual life seems impossible without friends to care for, bounce ideas off, worry about. My friendship with Jeff, I thought, demonstrated the powerful link between spirituality and the love of other people."[13]

Katz said that opportunities for friendship often come at critical times in our lives. He called those times "transitions—journeys of the soul." Someone dies. Someone moves. You have a child. You lose a job. You get sick. You get divorced. Moments that tear us open also often leave us ripe for new friendships that can help us heal and help us grow. I was struck by the depth and strength of another deep friendship between unrelated individuals when I read *A Life with Karol: My Forty-Year Friendship with the Man Who Became Pope*. The book chronicled the many years that Cardinal Stanislaw Dziwisz spent not only as Pope John Paul II's secretary and assistant, but also as his close personal friend and confidant.

The friendship began in 1966, when the man who would become a beloved pope, Karol Wojtyla, was the archbishop of Krakow, Poland. Archbishop Wojtyla asked Father Dziwisz to become his personal secretary even though Dziwisz had been ordained as a priest only three years earlier.

"As soon as I came in to see him, he looked straight at me and said, 'I'd like you to come live here. You can continue your studies and give me a hand.' 'When?' I asked. He replied, 'Today will work.' He turned toward the window and noticed that it was getting late. 'Go to the chancellor and he'll show you the room.' 'I'll come tomorrow,' I said. He watched me leave with a certain curiosity, but I noticed that he was smiling," Cardinal Dziwisz writes in the opening chapter of his book.[14]

Until then, the young priest had known Archbishop Wojtyla only from a distance, but as his secretary he began to get a closer, much more personal view of the man who would be pope. He noticed the deliberate and serious way he spoke the words of the Mass and the fact that he never celebrated Mass alone. He noticed the long periods of time he spent in silent prayer and the emphasis he placed on the graces received during confession.

Cardinal Dziwisz was there to observe and share in all of the details of the pope's public life, as well as many of his more private moments. This was the man who caught John Paul II's limp body after the pope was shot by a would-be assassin in 1981. He was there, too, when the pope forgave that shooter. He was there when the pope walked through the Brandenburg Gate after the fall of Communism. And he was there when the pope first watched the devastating footage of the fall of the Twin Towers in New York City. This friend was also there for the "secret" ski trips when the pope went skiing on the slopes in Austria, with no one the wiser. He was there when the pope prostrated himself on the floor of his private chapel, deep in prayer for hours at a time.

For forty years, Father Dziwisz kept not only the pope's calendar but his confidences. He listened to John Paul's thoughts, and, according to Cardinal Dziwisz, "a bit of his heart."[15] Although he spent much of his book recounting historical events that he witnessed at the pope's side, it is obvious that their working relationship was just one aspect of their lives together. Theirs was a deep friendship, a spiritual brotherhood that required no blood ties.

In one of the most moving passages, Cardinal Dziwisz recalled the moment when John Paul II died. "We were crying, of course. How could we have not cried? We were crying tears of grief and tears of joy at the same time. . . . I don't remember anything else after that. It's as if darkness suddenly descended on me and in me."[16]

In describing his final farewell to his beloved friend, Cardinal Dziwisz called it an "unforgettable event" and recalled that for twelve years in Krakow and for twenty-seven years in Rome, he had always been at the pope's side. "Now, in the moment of death, he'd gone on alone. I had accompanied him to a certain point, but then he'd gone on alone from there. And the fact that this time I wasn't able to accompany him hit me like a ton of bricks. . . . I did accompany him through an important stage of the Church's journey. But now he's gone on alone. And now? Who is accompanying him on the other side?"[17]

Cardinal Dziwisz's book is a moving memorial to the late pope, who was his spiritual friend in every sense of the word. It serves as a reminder to all of us that at any point in our lives—but often when we least expect it—we may come face to face with the person who will journey with us toward our spiritual home. After all, Cardinal Dziwisz was a young priest when the archbishop looked at him and said, "I'd like you to come live here."[18] He couldn't know then that the surprising but simple request would unfold as it did, completely changing his life, especially his spiritual life.

Food for Thought

1. Think about your own family relationships and whether there is someone in your family with whom you have shared a spiritual friendship. What is it about that relationship that sets it apart from your other family relationships?

2. If you are married, how do you and your spouse work toward building a spiritual friendship with each other

within your marriage? How might you encourage spiritual growth and prayer as a couple or family?

3. Reflect on any friends you have who are more like siblings than friends. How did that relationship develop and grow? How could you strengthen existing bonds to take that friendship to the next level by committing to a spiritual partnership?

Meditation

It is within the security and comfort
of our families that we first learn
what it means to love unconditionally,
to serve others in Christ-like fashion.
Today we pray for the ability to put aside
pettiness and personal gain in order to
develop more fully those friendships
that exist within our families of origin
as well as in our extended families of
relatives, friends, and neighbors.
It is among those with common interests,
common values, common goals that
we are likely to find holy friends
who understand our deepest needs,
our darkest fears, our greatest longings.

Chapter 7

Celibate Love:
A Different Kind of Passion

Consider the friendship that exists between women
and men, between men and women. Human nearness,
spiritual kinship, agreement in thoughts and feelings:
these are the foundations of friendship.

—Rudolf Schnackenburgh[1]

When Ed Mechmann first got to know Sister Mary Elizabeth, it was a casual friendship. They met at various pro-life events in and around the New York Archdiocese. But when she was assigned to head the archdiocesan Family Life/Respect Life Office, where Ed is associate director, things took a different turn. Ed says that there was a "sympathetic connection" between them, a "compatibility" that set their friendship apart from the kinds of friendships he had come to expect with other colleagues at work.

"Did you ever get that feeling when you meet someone that you're going to be friends with him or her? I just got that feeling with Sister Mary Elizabeth, that she was going to be an important person in my life, and it was meant to be that we would be friends," Ed says.

Ed is married and has three children, while Sister Mary Elizabeth is a New York-based Sister of Life. The two are spiritual friends, and theirs is a deep bond that is focused on a shared faith and a willingness to walk together on a spiritual path.

"If I were to say to anybody outside of my office or to someone like you, 'I love Sister Mary Elizabeth,' they would immediately think that it was sexual or romantic, and it's not. I think one of the things that liberates it to be more than that is the fact that I'm married and she's married, technically. We're in vowed relationships already, and because of that I feel very free with her, which can be difficult in other relationships," Ed explains. "I have friendships with people I work with and with other women, but it's different because there's always that element somewhere in the picture. But with this I feel very free because I don't have to pretend, and I don't have to worry, and I don't have to think about any of that stuff because that's not part of the relationship. It's not there, so I can just be myself."

Ed says that he saw something in Sister Mary Elizabeth that he desperately needed—a sense of peace and balance and a joyful spirituality lived out in the world day by day. It was the kind of spirituality and faith he was seeking in his own life.

"I am older than she is and in a very completely different way of life, obviously. She is immersed in the world of prayer, and I have to struggle to find time to pray, but what really gave me a real sense of intimacy in the right sense with her was just her spirituality. It's very simple and straightforward, and it was something that really attracted me. . . . She has a wonderful balance in her life, and it was something that I desperately needed in my life at the time," Ed explains. Ed believed that God put the friendship in his

life because he "needed to encounter" the kind of peaceful-
ness that Sister Mary Elizabeth exudes.

In Sister Mary Elizabeth, Ed witnessed a joyfulness he
had never experienced before. He learned to pray in new
ways, to see God as friend and partner by watching, listening, and sharing in Sister Mary Elizabeth's prayers. He saw
that Sister Mary Elizabeth always seemed to be in "some
level of communication with God" and began to realize
that even a "regular person" like himself could to do the
same. These two friends also prayed together in the more
traditional sense on a regular basis, strengthening their
friendship through their shared devotions.

"We pray the Angelus in the office at noon, we pray in
the car on the way to and from Albany, we pray the rosary
together. . . . It's the first relationship I've ever had aside
from the relationship I have with my wife where prayer is
actually part of the relationship," he says. "She has definitely helped me move forward on my spiritual path."

Going Against the Tide

Spiritual friendships like the one between Ed and Sister Mary
Elizabeth are unfortunately rare in our world today. We live
in an overly sexualized society. The laws of physical or sexual
attraction are used to sell everything from deodorant to breakfast cereal to blue jeans. So it's not surprising that our culture
can't seem to come to grips with male-female relationships
that do not have sexual overtones. Can't be done, people
say. There's no such thing as "just friends" when you're talking about men and women. Have we really reached a point
where men and women cannot interact on a deep and personal level without having it end in the bedroom?

Sexuality is a subject that is far more complicated than the overly sexualized and somewhat adolescent perspectives our society promotes as "normal." Sexual identity, of course, goes far beyond the laws of physical attraction. It includes not only our sexual desires, but also the innate qualities that make us men or women. For a woman, sexual identity might include a sense of nurturing. For a man, it might be an inclination to protect and defend others. In spiritual friendship, a man can benefit from a woman's perspective and vice versa. Their unique gifts can provide the friends with a viewpoint that they might not otherwise hear or see. Their differences can become strengths rather than obstacles to friendship.

Our society would lead us to believe that sexuality can lead to only one thing, but history shows us that when we live out our sexuality in healthy and chaste ways, it can actually lead to intimate but platonic friendships. We can develop friendships where true love is part of the equation despite the absence of a physical connection. Look at some of the greatest spiritual friendships in our faith history—Jesus and Mary Magdalene, Francis and Clare of Assisi, Francis de Sales and Jane de Chantal, and countless others. These were powerfully strong friendships. They were celibate friendships that reached a level of passion that had nothing to do with sexual attraction. Instead, they had everything to do with love—love of God and love for one another.

It is society's loss that relationships between men and women have been almost exclusively defined in terms of sexual behavior. While many marriages are spiritual friendships that allow both sexual and spiritual identities to exist side by side, it is also possible for unmarried "couples" to achieve deep spiritual friendships if they are willing to take on the challenges of developing male-female friendships "sans sex."

In his book *Forgotten Among the Lilies*, priest, author, and theologian Ronald Rolheiser says, "One of the deep wounds of Western culture is that men and women find it very hard to be friends. It's easy for them to be lovers, but not friends."[2]

Rolheiser is a member of the Missionary Oblates of Mary Immaculate and president of the Oblate School of Theology in San Antonio, Texas. He has written extensively about loneliness and isolation and about the obsessions that often control our lives. "Chaste, life-giving heterosexual friendship is rare," he writes, saying that we crave these kinds of friendships but often can't find them. When we do, we run up against the sexual tension that almost always goes hand-in-hand with male-female relationships of any kind. This happens not only because it is part of the way God made us, but because it is also part of the way our culture has made us.

"In our culture's view, a view we have generally interiorized and made our own, to love means to make love, to be a lover. Platonic heterosexual friendship is seen as too incomplete, too empty or as simply unrealistic," he wrote. "Heterosexual friendships require a delicate balance between caution and risk, between inhibition and daring vulnerability. But they are worth the risk and the effort."[3]

Let's go back again to some of those great male-female friendships from the annals of Church history. Society has even tried to sexualize them. How many modern movies and books have tried to turn Mary Magdalene into Jesus' lover or wife? The same holds true for St. Francis and Clare of Assisi. Some authors have twisted their story into a modern-day romance rather than show it for what it was, a spiritual friendship of the purest kind. Why? Because modern men and women have a hard time seeing those friendships outside the parameters of our sexualized cultural mindset. How could a man and woman love each other and not proceed to what has come to be seen as the next logical step: a sexual relationship?

In her book *The Cloister Walk*, author Kathleen Norris calls this male-female bond "celibate passion" and makes it clear that it is not always an easy path to walk. Norris, a Presbyterian who is also a Benedictine Oblate, shares the story of a priest with whom she developed a close friendship. She says that they were nearing the "rocky shoals of infatuation," an obstacle that had to be overcome if the friendship were to move in the right direction.

"The danger was real, but not insurmountable; I sensed that if our infatuation were to develop into love, that is, to ground itself in grace rather than utility, our respect for each other's commitments—his to celibacy, mine to monogamy —would make the boundaries of behavior very clear," she writes, saying that the friendship got them both through crises and propelled them forward in their prayer life.[4]

"This was celibacy at its best, a man's sexual energies so devoted to the care of others that a few words could lift me out of despair, give me the strength to reclaim my life," Norris continues. "Abundance indeed. Celibate love was at the heart of it, although I can't fully comprehend the mystery of why this should be so. Celibate passion—elusive, tensile, holy."[5]

Saintly Couples with a Passion

We can witness that celibate passion in some of the great spiritual couples we've already discussed. If you look at the letters of St. Francis de Sales to Jane de Chantal, you cannot help but hear the passion for their friendship in his "voice." The same holds true for another holy couple: Blessed Jordan of Saxony, who succeeded St. Dominic as master general of the Dominican Order, and Blessed Diana d'Andalo, who founded the contemplative Dominican convent of St. Agnes in Bologna.

Diana came from a wealthy family and was a friend of St. Dominic's. She wanted to be a nun, but her family objected. It was Blessed Jordan, also a good friend, who convinced her family to build a convent on their property so that Diana could fulfill her vocation while remaining close to home. Throughout the years of their friendship, Blessed Jordan's letters to Blessed Diana were filled not only with his love of God, but also with his love for Diana. Their "celibate passion" is obvious and touching:

"You are so deeply engraven on my heart, the more I realize how truly you love me from the depths of your soul. . . ." he wrote during the spring of 1228.[6]

Taken as it is, out of context, it's hard not to think of his prose as a love letter in the traditional sense, and yet, if you continue reading that same letter, it moves seamlessly into a prayer: "I must end this letter abruptly; but may he who is the supreme Consoler and Paraclete, the Spirit of Truth, possess and comfort your heart; and may he grant us to be with one another for ever in heavenly Jerusalem, through the grace of our Lord Jesus Christ who rules over all things, bless for ever. Amen."[7]

Within the pages and pages of letters that spanned their friendship, we can see a broad tapestry that includes threads of passion but also threads of prayer, greetings to Diana's sisters at the convent, and regards from the brothers traveling with Blessed Jordan. He addresses spiritual struggles, the prospect of war, the state of his health, and the state of his soul, and advises the sisters not to be overly stringent in the physical mortifications they practice. And yet always in the background is the passion that unites the two friends and keeps their bond strong even when they are separated by time and distance.

When you read the letters of Blessed Jordan and Diana, you recognize something deep and powerful and God-driven in everything that transpires between them. Their connection is not about wanting to be married to each other or to be joined in a sexual way; it is about wanting to achieve oneness with God and to spend eternity together in heaven (something we will address in the next chapter).

"The thought of you all rejoices my heart, beloved daughters, since I know how eagerly, in unity together, you walk with the Lord, seeking nothing save him in whom alone is your sufficiency . . ." Jordan wrote to Diana and her sisters in the summer of 1229.[8]

What Jordan shared with Diana is similar to what St. Francis de Sales shared with St. Jane de Chantal, and what St. Catherine of Siena shared with her spiritual director, confessor, and biographer, Blessed Raymond of Capua.

In *Saintly Companions*, author Vincent O'Malley writes: "Catherine wrote to Raymond about their 'close particular love' which 'cannot believe nor imagine that one of us wishes anything else than the other's good' while 'seeking ever in the other the glory of the name of God and the profit of his holy soul.'"[9]

That is what celibate passion between a man and a woman is all about: it seeks goodness and holiness for the spiritual friend-partners in a way that ignites their souls and leads them onward toward heaven, renewed and re-energized by the holy friendship they share.

Catherine was born the youngest of twenty-five children in 1347. She joined the Dominicans at age sixteen and was a mystic, a counselor to popes, and a stigmatic. She is recognized as a Doctor of the Church. Her visions and supernatural gifts caused discord among some of the sisters in her community, and she was forced to go to Florence to defend herself against charges before a general chapter of Dominicans. She was cleared of any wrongdoing and assigned a spiritual director: Blessed Raymond, who would become a trusted friend and guide.

Throughout her life, Catherine was powerful and fearless in her love of God and the Church. It isn't really surprising, then, that such a spiritually passionate person would bring that same depth and devotion to her closest friendships. We are, after all, the sum of our parts. We cannot discard passion and check it at the door simply because we have developed a close friendship with someone of the opposite sex. What must happen instead is that we manage our passion, in a sense. We remain ever vigilant in keeping our physical passions and weaknesses in check, and redirect our energies and passions toward spirituality, goodness, and Godliness.

Celibate Passion in a Sexual World

Obviously, having a close relationship with a member of the opposite sex who is not your wife, husband, or significant other is not without risks. People will wonder. You may even wonder yourself if you find yourself in a male-female spiritual friendship. After all, if society says that this kind of celibate passion cannot really exist, who are you to disagree? Disagree, but be wary.

If you are trying to fill a void in your own life perhaps because of an unhappy marriage, failed marriage, loneliness, or some other unhappiness, you cannot develop a true spiritual friendship with a member of the opposite sex. It is a recipe for disaster. These types of relationships are already fraught with issues put on them from the outside world. If you come into a spiritual friendship with your own interior issues, searching for someone to fill a particular need, things are bound to go awry. You could easily find yourself in an unhealthy dependency or even in an adulterous affair.

Spiritual friendships between men and women have to exist within emotionally and spiritually healthy lives, healthy marriages, and healthy vocations. In fact, if a married man or woman wants to maintain a spiritual friendship with a member of the opposite sex who is not a spouse, that person's marriage must be honest, faith-filled, and stronger than average. Even in the best marriages, a spouse who has a spiritual friend of the opposite sex should be prepared for potential jealousy and concern on the part of the other spouse. After all, a deep emotional attachment to someone outside the marriage partnership can be viewed as a threat, even when a marriage is on solid ground. Remember to be aware of those potential issues, to honor the feelings of your spouse, and to be willing to rein in the spiritual friendship if it threatens to cause an upheaval in your marriage. The bottom line is that no spiritual friendship should ever damage the relationship between a husband and wife.

As mentioned previously, I have a close spiritual friendship with Bill, a priest I met many years ago when I first began working for the Church. Our friendship now includes my husband and children, but it also exists on its own spiritual plane. Bill may come over for dinner and hang out with the family, watching movies with us or playing with the kids in the backyard. But, in addition to that, he and I also spend a lot of time, mostly by phone or through e-mail, discussing our spiritual journeys. We talk about where we are, where we want to be, the struggles we encounter, the doubts or darkness we may feel, as well as the moments of spiritual joy we may experience in prayer.

It is a very special relationship, but it could not exist if I did not have a strong, loving, and honest relationship with my husband, Dennis. We have talked openly about my friendship with Bill, about what it means and how it is possible for me to have a male friend who will not endanger my marriage. And it is possible because Bill and I have also discussed our commitments to our own vocations. We can both see how our deep friendship can actually build up our individual vocations and strengthen them by strengthening our individual connections to God.

Doesn't it make sense that we would have spiritual friends of both sexes during our lives? We are drawn to people because of common interests, similar spiritual styles, and shared goals. It is only natural that sometimes those friends will be of the opposite sex. Those kinds of friendships can bring with them new insights and untold blessings. But we tend to shy away from these friendships out of fear or confusion. Or, we can fall prey to the cultural trap or sexual attraction, allowing a wonderful friendship to go off course, moving away from the spiritual toward the physical.

If we approach male-female friendships from a spiritual plane, grounding them, as Kathleen Norris says, in "grace rather than utility," we can share in the kind of spiritual life partnerships that sometimes seem confined to saints of bygone eras.[10]

What does it mean to ground a friendship in "grace rather than utility"? It means that we pray and focus our energies on God and spiritual growth, not on what will benefit us most or make us—even temporarily—satisfied or happy. Spiritual friendship is not about feeding our own human needs. It is about finding a way to transcend the "typical" stuff of male-female relationships in order to rest together in a grace-filled place where God is always at the center.

By anchoring our male-female friendships in God and using the saints as guides, we can walk the path of celibate love in proud defiance of modern cultural attitudes toward sexuality. And, as we reap the many blessings those friendships provide, we can bring those blessings to bear in our families and our world.

Food for Thought

1. Reflect on any friendships—spiritual or otherwise— that you have shared with someone of the opposite sex without any expectation of a physical relationship.

What were the difficulties in maintaining such a friendship? What were the blessings and benefits?

2. Look at some of the great saint "couples." How might you use these men and women to guide or nurture your own spiritual friendship with someone of the opposite sex?

3. If you are married, think about some ways that you might keep your spiritual friendship from becoming an issue in your marriage. What do you need to discuss with your spouse and spiritual friend to ensure that the friendship remains "intimate" in the right sense?

Meditation

Despite what our modern culture
preaches about sexuality and love,
we recognize and celebrate the fact
that deep and powerful friendships
can exist between men and women
who remain focused on God.
Today we pray for the courage
to open our hearts to
celibate passion, celibate love,
to be aware that these friendships
bring challenges as well as blessings,
risks as well as benefits.
By journeying together in grace,
may we discover a new way
to relate, a new way to grow,
a new way to meet God on
the path to spiritual wholeness.

Chapter 8

Commitment:
A Connection That Even
Death Cannot Part

A person without a Soul Friend is like a body without a head.

—St. Brigid of Ireland

Donna-Marie Cooper O'Boyle was trying to help a friend in crisis when she sought out the guidance of a spiritual director, Jesuit Father John A. Hardon. She spoke with him by phone and then went to Georgetown University, where he was stationed at the time, to meet with him in person. Donna brought her family with her on the journey from her home in Connecticut. She did not realize then that this first meeting would lead to a deep friendship and a lasting bond with the priest whose cause for beatification is now under way.

"Father Hardon directed me spiritually from the moment I was first in touch with him. We stayed in touch by phone and mail, and I attended many of his retreats over the years as well as spent time with him at the Missionaries of Charity convents where he gave retreats to the Sisters. We became close, and a friendship developed," says Donna, who asked Father Hardon to be godfather to her youngest daughter,

121

Mary-Catherine. "Father Hardon's friendship ultimately in-spired me to go on to do many things," she said.

Through Father Hardon's friendship, Donna met Blessed Mother Teresa of Calcutta and became a lay Mis-sionary of Charity. She even founded a branch of that order in Connecticut.

"Father Hardon's spiritual direction was powerful since he was an extremely holy man. I really believe that Father Hardon's friendship and spiritual direction prodded me on to all faith-related things and also inspired my writings," Donna said.

Although Father Hardon died in 2000, Donna still feels connected with him—as she does with Father William C. Smith, another spiritual director and close friend for more than twenty-five years.

"I call upon them frequently now to watch over my family. My two—three if we include Blessed Mother Teresa —spiritual mentors and friends have gone on to their eter-nal reward but are still close to my heart and soul. I speak to and call upon them often for their intercession," she says.

What Donna experienced in her close friendships with her spiritual directors and mentors, and what she continues to experience now, even after their deaths, is a distinctive characteristic of spiritual friendship. These kinds of deep friendships never end. Even when one friend dies, the re-lationship continues through prayer and the ties that only faith can provide. It is permanent, everlasting, etched on our souls for all time.

Maybe Some Things Aren't Temporary

In a line from one of my favorite movies, *Moonstruck*, the main character, Loretta, points to a man's pinkie ring she was given during a marriage proposal and says to her stunned and annoyed father, "It's temporary." At which point her father yells back, "Everything is temporary!" And therein lies the problem with so much of our world today. Everything is temporary, or so it seems.

Look around your own home and consider how many things are "disposable." Although we're more focused on living "green" lives these days, the reality is that we like to be able to change things. It could be the curtains in the living room or the cell phone plan that's just been purchased. Or, it could be the computer that seems to be obsolete even before it's out of the packaging.

Relationships, too, can seem temporary or disposable these days. Half of all marriages end in divorce. Young people are content to "hook up" rather than build serious and satisfying connections with a deeply loved person. We live in a culture that wants to keep its options open.

The bond of spiritual friendship, however, is not temporary, disposable, or broken by the force of death. It is an eternal commitment, something that is foreign to our worldview. How can friendship continue for all eternity? What does that even mean? In what capacity can spiritual friends expect to maintain a relationship when one or both have moved on to the next life, a life we have not yet glimpsed or experienced?

In his book *The Catholic Passion: Rediscovering the Power and Beauty of the Faith*, author David Scott captures this belief in the interconnectedness of all beings, even across the divide of heaven and earth.

"Our relationships with those on earth are not severed once we reach heaven. On earth, we benefit from the holiness and love of the saints in heaven. They look out for us, listen to our prayers, intercede for us. In heaven we too will assume responsibility for caring and praying for the ones we leave behind. . . . From heaven we will watch over our brothers and sisters on earth, especially our loved ones. We will experience their joys and their sorrows, with ears open always to their pleas and petitions."[1]

Our faith reminds us that this life is part of a continuum. We will go forward from here to be with God, with the angels and saints, and with those we have loved. And so, as we build up deep friendships here on earth, friendships rooted in faith, we can take comfort in knowing that what we begin in our earthly life will continue in the next.

The late theologian Henri J. M. Nouwen talked about the reality of such lasting friendships in his book *Life of the Beloved*, when he shared the pain of losing two dear friends. "I miss them. Their deaths are a painful loss. Whenever I think of them, I feel the biting pain that they are no longer in their homes with their families and friends. I can no longer call them, visit them, hear their voices or see their faces. I feel immense grief. But I believe that their deaths are more than a loss. Their deaths are also a gift."[2]

He went on to explain: "The deaths of those whom we love and who love us open up the possibility of a new, more radical communion, a new intimacy, a new belonging to each other. If love is, indeed, stronger than death, then death has the potential to deepen and strengthen the bonds of love."[3]

Spiritual friendship doesn't follow worldly guidelines; it follows God's plan. And, as we know, God's plan does not have an expiration date. It goes on forever in a way that we humans cannot really fathom. Friendship that is rooted in God is part of that heavenly plan. We can see that truth repeated in the writings of Nouwen, the saints, and scripture itself.

Think about Jesus at the Last Supper, when he gathered with the apostles. He told them not to let their hearts be troubled by the thought that he was leaving them. "In my Father's house there are many dwelling places. If there were not, would I have told you that I am going to prepare a place for you? And if I go and prepare a place for you, I will come back again and take you to myself, so that where I am you also may be" (Jn 13:2–3).

Jesus promises to take his friends with him into eternity. In that promise, spiritual friends can recognize an echo of what they can expect to share. Spiritual friendship is not tied to earthly gains and progress. It is not about stockpiling material things or reaching a particular set of human goals and objectives. It is about walking together on a path that leads to heaven. It is only logical—if faith can ever be logical—to conclude that a friendship whose one goal is union with God for all eternity would continue to exist in that spiritual realm until the end of time.

Eternity: A Definition

If you think about it, eternity doesn't always seem so wonderful, does it? When we say that an event went on "for an eternity," we usually don't mean that in a positive way. We think of eternity and imagine ourselves plodding on and on as we do now with no end in sight. It doesn't necessarily seem like the most satisfying goal, even as we continue to strive for it. Eternity is not something our human minds can grasp. That makes it that much harder for us to grasp the notion of eternal friendship.

Let's talk about eternity in general before we talk about eternal friendship more specifically. Pope Benedict XVI, in his encyclical *Spe Salvi* (Saved in Hope), said that we humans are driven toward an unknown "true life" that we don't understand and yet crave. The "unknown" aspect of eternal life can at once give us hope and drive us to despair.

"The term 'eternal life' is intended to give a name to this 'unknown.' Inevitably it is an inadequate term that creates confusion. 'Eternal,' in fact, suggests to us the idea of something interminable. This frightens us. 'Life' makes us think of the life that we know and love and do not want to lose, even though very often it brings more toil than satisfaction. On the one hand, we desire it, but on the other hand, we do not want it," Pope Benedict writes. "To imagine ourselves outside the temporality that imprisons us and in some way to sense that eternity is not an unending succession of days in the calendar, but something more like the supreme moment of satisfaction, in which totality embraces us and we embrace totality—this we can only attempt. It would be like plunging into the ocean of infinite love, a moment in which time—the before and after—no longer exists."[4]

So how does this "unknown" hope of eternal life, then, impact our spiritual friendships in a real way? Are there certain requirements that must be met to earn this eternal prize? Is there an instruction manual that we need to memorize? If we are lucky enough to find ourselves in a deep spiritual friendship, the eternal quality of it really takes care of itself.

We must first commit ourselves to all the things we've already discussed—unconditional love, virtue, communication, and, above all, a life focused on God. If those things remain central to our spiritual friendship, they will allow the relationship to defy the limits of time and space and extend to places that we only dare to imagine at this point.

St. Francis de Sales tells us: "Truly it is a blessed thing to love on earth as we hope to love in Heaven, and to begin that friendship here which is to endure forever there."[5]

The recognition of this eternal quality in our spiritual friendships can help us forge deeper bonds with and stronger commitments to those who are our "soul twins," our sacred companions on earth. We can look forward and realize that the friendship that strengthens us and brings us back when we begin to drift will remain even after one or both of the friends are gone. We can take comfort in knowing that a spiritual energy and the power of prayer can link us even when we cannot pick up a telephone or dash off an e-mail. It is a powerful thing to think of a relationship lasting endlessly into the future. It flies in the face of human reason, and it overturns the idea that "everything is temporary."

Aelred of Rievaulx, the twelfth-century Cistercian monk who explored this subject at length in his book *Spiritual Friendship*, says that God's gift of friendship between people who love each other as they love themselves leads to eternal friendship.

"There one finds no hiding of thoughts, no dissembling of affection. This is true and eternal friendship, which begins in this life and is perfected in the next, which here belongs to the few where few are good, but there belongs to all where all are good," he wrote.[6]

This idea of eternal friendship really ties together all of the things we've been talking about up until this point. If we commit ourselves to spiritual friendships grounded in grace and prayer, humility and charity, openness and honesty, we begin to build something here on earth that carries the spark of eternity within it.

From Here to Eternity

When I think about this eternal aspect of spiritual friendship, I cannot help but reflect on my relationship with my mother. Because she was my first spiritual friend and because she died so many years ago, our ongoing connection gives some weight to this idea of eternal bonds that exist between spiritual friends.

I'm not saying that I have some sort of psychic connection with my dead mother. I do not. I hardly ever even dream about her or "feel" her presence. Our connection is strictly spiritual. Many years after her death, I never really feel far from my mother. The lessons she imparted, the wisdom she shared, the spiritual life that was central to her daily existence remain with me as I go about my own life. At times I will recall something she said, or something she did that impressed and continues to guide me.

Certain people come into our lives, and their friendships leave indelible marks. Their friendships are like spiritual tattoos—beautiful tattoos—that never fade. Close family members are the most likely candidates when it comes to this sort of cosmic connection, but spiritual friends can similarly have a deep and lasting impact that stretches beyond earth's physical boundaries.

I had a close friend named Rob, who died far too young—just shy of his thirty-sixth birthday. When Rob and I first became friends, I was definitely in the spiritual mentor role. He would call me when he wanted someone to go with him to Mass or to take out a guitar and sing religious songs. And for me he was a fashion mentor, taking me shopping or cutting my hair in my family's kitchen at home long before he opened his own hair salon. Much to my mother's chagrin, he would stand there, smiling and snipping away at my curls, saying, "Times are changing and so is Mar!"

Rob was always a little bit different in all the best ways. He was a real sweetheart with a quick smile, a generous heart, and a willingness to overlook other people's faults. He had his share of hard times in life, but he always landed on his feet and ended up a better person for it.

I'll never forget the day I sat in a chair at his salon as he styled my hair. Over the din of the blow dryer, he told me he was gay. And although it didn't really come as a surprise, I remember the moment like it was yesterday. It was a defining moment, an honest moment in our friendship. Rob was telling me that he really understood who he was. He was happy, and I was happy for him.

Through some very long separations our friendship remained strong. When I lived across the country, it wouldn't surprise me to come home and find a sweet, singing message from Rob. He would leave a few bars from Stevie Wonder's "I Just Called to Say I Love You" on my answering machine. He was like an extra younger brother who popped in and out of my life but always, always stayed in my heart.

Then Rob got cancer. Even then he kept up a good front, so good that I didn't realize how ill he was until he was gone. After Rob died, his sister Colleen talked to me about Rob's final moments. It seems that as he was about to enter eternity, he told family members and friends gathered around him that my mother was present and was beckoning him. She was comforting him and telling him that everything was going to be okay. Although he did not have a particularly close relationship with my mother, it did not surprise me to think that she would somehow be present to Rob in a motherly way as he prepared to leave this world.

Many years after Rob's death, I occasionally feel his presence in my life. I have had distinct "Rob moments." One day, for instance, I opened up a dust-covered prayer book sitting untouched on a shelf only to have Rob's prayer card drop out. It was the anniversary of his death and I had completely forgotten it. I have also felt Rob's presence at times that were unconnected to a birthday or anniversary. At those times, I have wondered why the connection seemed so strong. Was there a memory or lesson from my friendship with Rob that was meant to influence my life at that moment?

It is a fleeting feeling that can make me smile, cry, laugh, or turn up the car radio to sing a song that Rob loved. Regardless of my reaction, the reality is that we still have a connection all these years later. I foolishly gave up the opportunity to see Rob one more time before he died, not realizing his condition was as serious as it turned out to be. I never forgave myself for that, but apparently Rob did.

From a human perspective, it can be hard to see how friendships in this life might continue into the next. But when we look at the people closest to us who have already gone home to God, we can sometimes catch glimpses of eternity. Those glimpses come in ordinary coincidences in which we encounter memories of our loved ones washing back onto the shores of our souls. The "ocean of infinite love" laps at our feet. We are reminded that while everything is temporary here on earth, nothing is temporary where God is concerned.

Last Word

At the end of one of my favorite children's books, *Charlotte's Web*, Wilbur the pig confronts the grim news that his "true friend," Charlotte, is going to die and will not return to their shared barn with her babies.

Wilbur, who has been spared the smokehouse and a place of honor on the Christmas dinner platter thanks to Charlotte's handiwork, asked: "Why did you do all this for me? . . . I've never done anything for you."

"You have been my friend," replied Charlotte. "That in itself is a tremendous thing. I wove my webs for you because I like you. . . . By helping you, perhaps I was trying to lift up my life a trifle. Heaven knows anyone's life can stand a little of that."

Wilbur told Charlotte that she saved him, adding, "I would gladly give my life for you—I really would."[7]

Then Wilbur took charge of Charlotte's egg sac, returning it safely to their barn and protecting it until the spiders hatched and flew off on the sticky webs—except for three who remained there with Wilbur to continue Charlotte's lineage in the barn doorway. We are told later that although Wilbur had many new friends, none of them ever took the place of Charlotte in his heart.

So, even in one of the most famous barnyards in children's literature, we find useful lessons about spiritual friendship. *Charlotte's Web* is a story of unconditional love, of friendship grounded in giving first to the other, no matter what the cost. It may have been written for children, but Wilbur and Charlotte's story is our story. It is the story of two unlikely friends who find each other in the most unexpected places and develop a deep and abiding relationship not grounded in claims to power and glory, but rooted in humility, love, and charity. When those virtues combine at the heart of a spiritual friendship, an eternal bond is forged.

Food for Thought

1. How do you view eternity? Do you fear it even as you strive for it? Can you describe what it is that you fear?

2. Can you think of ways that you have experienced an "eternal" connection with someone who has died? Was

there an event or words shared with you that may have
seemed ordinary at the time but extraordinary now?

3. St. Francis de Sales and Aelred of Rievaulx both talked
    about beginning a spiritual friendship on earth and
    perfecting it in heaven. What does that mean to you?
    How might you nourish your earthly friendships in
    ways that will allow them to flourish for all eternity?

Meditation

It is difficult for us to wrap
our human minds around
God's promise of eternity.
We want to fit eternity into
our own definition of time,
but God is not constrained by
earthly limitations.
God offers something beyond
what we can imagine.
Today we pray for the openness
to dare to imagine what God
has in store for us and those friends
who walk with us in his sight.
We take comfort in the knowledge
that we will not face an eternity
in isolation but in constant connection
to all those who loved and served God
alongside us here on earth.

Chapter 9

Community:
Finding and Keeping
Soul Friends

A friend is long sought, hardly found, and with difficulty kept.

—St. Jerome

I belong to a very large parish in upstate New York. Without exaggeration, I can say that it took me years to feel at home in this parish. It wasn't because there weren't nice people to be found. It was simply because in a parish with thousands of families, newcomers can feel a little lost in the crowd. Finally I realized that if I didn't jump in and join a parish organization, I would always feel like an outsider in my own church. So, I signed up to help with a few ministries. Before I knew it, I was a fixture at the parish center. I met a lot of wonderful people, but I had not yet made any deeper connections.

Then one day I was at our parish picnic and noticed a woman with very curly hair. She was standing nearby with her three daughters. I walked up to her and asked who cut her hair. I, too, have very curly hair and am always in the market for a good stylist. Our brief and funny conversation was the beginning of a beautiful friendship. Although we spoke for only a few minutes that day, we met again in our parish Gathering Space after Mass one week. Then we offered to run a preschool workshop together at our parish's Generations of Faith program. Before long, we were meeting weekly to read the Sunday scriptures with other moms during Lent and singing in our parish's Contemporary Choir. Most of all, we were enjoying the fact that we had found each other unexpectedly there in the bright sunshine of our town park on a September afternoon.

More recently, Michele and I attended a women's retreat sponsored by our parish. When I first signed up to attend the Women's Cornerstone Retreat, I thought it would serve as a warm-up to a "real" retreat later in the year. I hadn't been on a retreat since high school. I figured Cornerstone would be a good way to get my feet wet and connect with some women at the same time. What unfolded, however, went far beyond my wildest dreams. The twenty-six hours spent at the Carondelet Hospitality Center in Latham, New York, was a gift and a blessing.

For the first time since joining my large suburban parish seven years earlier, I felt as though I had finally found the small faith community I was searching for.

I was humbled and awestruck by the deep faith and wisdom of the women on this retreat. Ranging from "thirty-something" to those in their eighties, these women had an obvious hunger to move deeper into their spiritual journey, and it made me want to stand up and shout for joy. I had been struggling to find a way to move forward on my own faith journey despite the busyness and stress of everyday life. Right here in my own backyard were dozens of other women who wanted the very same thing.

Through powerful witness talks, honest and tear-filled conversations, prayer, and song, we went from being strangers to sisters in a matter of hours. As we sat at the closing Mass on Saturday night, I looked around again. Surely, this was what it must have been like to be a faith community in the early days of the Church. These women were sharing their experiences, their joys, and their sorrows, all in the context of a Christ-centered faith that was the foundation of their lives.

This retreat took place at a hospitality center based at the provincial house of the Sisters of St. Joseph of Carondelet. Those on retreat were assured of the prayers of the 175 sisters who lived there. We said Morning Prayer with the sisters, ate with them in their cafeteria, and held a prayer circle outside their chapel as they walked or were wheeled into Mass. Their presence, interwoven into the rhythm of our retreat, made it that much more special. At one point, as I sat outside the chapel, an older sister walked over to me, took my hand, and reminded me that all of the sisters had been praying for us and would continue to do so. "It doesn't end when you leave here," she said. "You are trapped in our prayers." That alone made the entire weekend worth the effort it took to get there.

In the end, this weekend was about community, about faith, about finding other women who wanted to journey together toward God. It was the beginning of something monumental for the women of my parish. That original retreat group has blossomed. Women from the first retreat sponsored a second retreat the next year, and plans are already underway for the third retreat. In addition, the larger group, which now includes women from both retreats, continues to meet and to grow together spiritually.

"For me, the beauty of this weekend lies in the fact that now when I see you in church, I will see more than a face and a smile. I will see and know your heart," said my Cornerstone sister Claire, in a comment on a blog post I had written about the retreat. My friend Michele added: "Even the disciples were told by Jesus to go out 'two by two' because he knew they couldn't do it alone. The Cornerstone retreat was the beginning of something wonderful, and I was blessed to share it with you."

"I knew that I would enjoy this weekend. Liz reminded me that I had said 'yes' immediately when she told me about the retreat. I didn't expect, however, for it to be life-changing. I have never felt as connected to so many other women," wrote Natalie, another of my Cornerstone sisters. "I believe that the Holy Spirit worked his way through us, and we are bound to each other now through our words, and embraces, and tears, and prayers. What a beautiful experience! What a precious gift!"

From this brief retreat, a community of spiritual friends has been born. This was certainly a case of God leading us to each other. None of us knew what to expect when we sent in that retreat registration form. Many of us wondered what we were doing there when we had husbands and children and responsibilities waiting at home. But after the laughter and tears, prayers and songs, we had made a spiritual connection that is real and lasting. Even when I see a Cornerstone sister in the grocery store, we can't help but hug and, without saying a word, remember that faith-filled weekend that brought us together.

Where Two or Three Are Gathered . . .

When we think about nurturing a deep spiritual life, many of us often conjure up secluded chapels or quiet monasteries where we could spend hours in solitude and silent contemplation. I know I do. After all, how can we walk the path of spiritual growth in our daily lives when that path is strewn with responsibilities and chores? As we commute to work or shuttle children from one activity to another, it is easy to assume that the only way to make real spiritual progress is to break away from the crowd and turn our spiritual quests into solo flights. But if we look at the history of the Church, from the days of Jesus onward, it's clear that isolation is not the spiritual oasis it first appears to be. We need like-minded friends. We need community.

Jesus went out into the desert alone to pray at times. But it was in community with his apostles and disciples that he spent the bulk of his time. With his brothers and sisters nearby, Jesus broke bread, cast out demons, taught in parables, performed miracles, changed lives. When he was headed to the Garden of Gethsemane, Jesus took along some of his disciples and said to them: "My soul is sorrowful even to death. Remain here and keep watch with me" (Mt 26:38). In the prelude to his darkest hour, Jesus did not want to be alone. Although he went off by himself to pray, he kept his community of friends nearby for support and strength and comfort.

And so it is with us. We can and should disappear now and then—to a prayer space within our home or a quiet corner of our parish church, or even a hermitage or retreat center for an extended period of prayer. But that is not the norm for us, and we should never expect it to be. The norm for those of us walking this spiritual path toward God out in the world is found in friendship, in community with those who share our spiritual longings.

"For as in one body we have many parts, and all the parts do not have the same function, so we, though many, are one body in Christ and individually parts of one another," St. Paul said in his Letter to the Romans (Rom 12:4–5). We are not meant to strive for heaven confined to our own little individual spiritual cocoons. We are meant to strive together, leaning on each other, nudging each other forward, strengthening the larger community through our individual gifts and talents—hand in hand, heart to heart, soul to soul.

When we do look at monks and cloistered nuns living in small, silent cells, it becomes clear that community is central even in their lives. Although monks may spend hours in the seclusion of their cells, they come together to pray, to chant, to celebrate Mass, to work, and to share meals. We can thank St. Benedict for this emphasis on community life.

"Benedictine spirituality is unique in the strong emphasis it places on love in community. It is the primary vow of stability that defines the Benedictine community as a loving family. Here love becomes concrete and not simply a spiritual abstract," wrote Brian C. Taylor in *Spirituality for Everyday Living: An Adaptation of the Rule of St. Benedict.*

"Relationships have a singularly important role in the Benedictine way of life."[1]

This community life is marked by humility, obedi-
ence, a respectful attitude toward each member, and, of
course, spiritual growth through communal prayer, but
also through silent and personal prayer. St. Benedict's focus
was balanced. We can learn a lot from his message of doing
things in moderation, of incorporating work and prayer into
the day, of welcoming every person as if Christ was coming
into our midst. Although we may each have a personal relationship with Jesus Christ, we are not meant to keep that
relationship to ourselves. We are called to share the Good
News, to join our voices in prayer, to work together for the
greater good. In short, we are called to be brothers and sisters in Christ, spiritual friends on a spiritual mission.

Seek and You Shall Find

Where are we to find spiritual friends who will band together with us? It's not always easy to know. In our scattered
and high-speed world, finding even one spiritual friend, no
less a community of spiritual friends, can be a challenge.
But if we know where to look, it becomes possible, even
probable.

You may already belong to a parish or church. That's
the first place to begin making connections. I'm not talking about just shaking hands across the pews at the Sign
of Peace or chatting over a cup of coffee during fellowship.
I'm talking about real connections. Strike up a conversation,
join a scripture study group, volunteer to run a food drive
or help with the parish picnic. It doesn't have to be a wholly

spiritual event to lead you to a spiritual friend. The back-drop of faith there in your local church is enough to give you common ground, a starting point.

The only way to make connections in a parish setting is to get involved on a personal level. Then you can take bigger strides toward something deeper. Maybe you can go on a parish retreat or join a small faith community. Perhaps the group that knits shawls for the local nursing home would like to incorporate some prayer and reflection, giving the ready-made community a spiritual dimension.

The most obvious place to begin to build a community of spiritual friends is within your existing church community or through a regional church organization. These are people who already share your faith. Surely within that group you can find one or two people who not only share your beliefs, but perhaps your sense of humor or your appreciation for history or your love of religious art. Look around and be open. Remember, a "community" does not have to be a crowd. Jesus said, "For where two or three are gathered together in my name, there am I in the midst of them" (Mt 18:20).

Don't forget that sometimes a friend will find you when you least expect it. My friend Michele would say that's not a coincidence but a "God-incidence," meaning that there was nothing random about an unlikely meeting or friendship. C. S. Lewis in *The Four Loves* echoes that sentiment. He says that unlike other relationships, where we think we are the ones doing the picking and choosing, Christian friendships are not our doing but God's.

"But, for a Christian, there are strictly speaking, no chances. A secret Master of Ceremonies has been at work. Christ, who said to the disciples, 'Ye have not chosen me, but I have chosen you,' can truly say to every group of Christian friends, 'You have not chosen one another but I have chosen you for one another.' The friendship is not a reward for our discrimination and good taste in finding one another out. It is the instrument by which God reveals to each the beauties of all the others."[2]

Just because God may be doing the choosing for us, that doesn't mean we don't have a role to play. Did you ever hear that joke about the guy who keeps praying to win the lottery and one day asks God why he has forsaken him? God responds: "Meet me halfway on this one. Buy a ticket!" Well, we have to meet God halfway and buy a ticket. Sometimes, we're going to find a spiritual friend out of the clear blue sky. But most of the time we're going to have to take an active part in putting ourselves out there and meeting people with whom we just might "click."

Of course, sometimes our community is spread out across the country or state. We may have spiritual friends who share our common interests and goals but live hours away. We can create a sense of community even from a distance by trying to foster spiritual activities that will bridge the gap when we are apart.

And one final word on where to find a community of spiritual friends—the family. The family is the domestic church, and it's the perfect place to begin building a community of spiritual friends. You can mark your days with the rhythm of shared prayers and rituals. You can balance solitude and community, a balance that the monastics have long understood as vital to spiritual growth. What better place to nurture a community of spiritual friends than there among the people we love the most?

On the Streets of New York

I think sometimes when we look at the lives of the great saint friends, it's hard to imagine ourselves in their place. Surely, St. Francis and St. Clare of Assisi are wonderful role models, but they seem so far from us. They lived in another time, another world. How can we hope to achieve what they did? What we need to remember is that we are not expected to recreate the lives or friendships of those holy men and women who came before us. We are meant to take comfort and strength from what they experienced and apply what we can to our own lives. Still, maybe it would help if we looked at someone closer to our own time and place, someone like Dorothy Day.

Dorothy Day founded the Catholic Worker movement and lived a life in solidarity with the poorest of the poor. She had a tumultuous past—a forced abortion, a lovechild with an intellectual elitist who had no need for God or religion, and a fierce commitment to work for justice and the poor even when it landed her in jail repeatedly. One day in 1932, she was in Washington, DC, reporting on a hunger march when she went to the Shrine of the Immaculate Conception and prayed that "some way would open up for me to use what talents I possessed for my fellow workers, for the poor."[3] When she returned home to New York City, Peter Maurin, the Frenchman who would become her partner in the Catholic Worker movement, was waiting on her doorstep.

In the introduction to the book *Dorothy Day: Selected Writings*, editor Robert Ellsberg wrote about the fact that Day and Maurin were an unlikely match, although they had similar ideas. "This was true in the sense that they were both searching for a way to relate their faith to the urgent social issues of the day. Otherwise it would be hard to imagine two less likely collaborators," Ellsberg wrote, explaining that Maurin was twenty years older than Day, came from another time and culture, and took his cues from Medieval Irish monks. Day, on the other hand, was "restless and impatient" and very American in her view of the day's class struggles.[4]

"Both would have to do some adjusting. Nevertheless, even before they had met, Peter Maurin was confident that Providence had ordained the partnership," says Ellsberg.[5]

Writing about Maurin, Day said: "Peter made you feel a sense of mission as soon as you met him . . . he aroused in you a sense of your own capacities for work, for accomplishment. He made you feel that you and all men had great and generous hearts with which to love God."[6] She talked about her working relationship with him, saying, "It was amazing how little we understood each other at first. But Peter was patient. . . . It was always with humor, never with bitterness or malice, that we differed."[7]

Day and Maurin were unlikely friends brought together because of their shared commitment to the Church and the gospel and the least of their brothers and sisters. They were collaborators who instilled a sense of mission in one another, even when they didn't always agree on specifics. They disagreed, as all friends do from time to time. But they always disagreed with respect and humor. They expanded their relationship outward to encompass and engage others in their work and their spiritual journey.

Author Marc H. Ellis, in an essay titled "Peter Maurin: To Bring the Social Order to Chaos," called the Maurin-Day friendship and partnership "providential." Ellis said that their backgrounds and gifts were complementary despite their vastly different experiences.

"The prophetic quality of their encounter can be measured by the depth of their spiritual calling: their readiness to abandon self; their ability to stand in opposition to the present as they affirmed a future; their will to persevere in success and failure; their inclusion of others in the search for personal and social salvation," Ellis wrote in the essay (included in the book *Revolution of the Heart*).[8]

Dorothy Day and Peter Maurin were spiritual friends, companions on a journey that found its common starting point in God. Their common vision and faith allowed them to overcome superficial differences to strive for something deeper, more meaningful and lasting.

That is what spiritual friendships can do. They can bring together people from different backgrounds who share a common vision, a common faith, a common goal. We may look at a person across the pews from us at church and see someone who seems unlike us. But thrown together because of a common interest or because of "coincidence," we often find that we are more alike than we are different. We realize that we want the same things in our spiritual lives and that we enjoy having company—community—for the journey.

Community of Two: Spiritual Director as Spiritual Friend

Spiritual direction is not going to guarantee you spiritual friendship. However, it is a good place to begin or expand your spiritual quest. Whether you already have a spiritual director or are in search of one, you are in good company. Many of the great saints who went before you received ongoing spiritual direction throughout their lives. Finding a director who can guide you on your path and give you advice when it comes to prayer, contemplation, and spiritual reading is always a good thing. If you are truly blessed, your spiritual director may become a spiritual friend. You should never go into a spiritual direction relationship expecting a spiritual friendship, but be open to that possibility.

If we look at many historical examples of spiritual friendships, it's obvious that many of them started out within the framework of spiritual direction. Francis of Assisi and Clare, Francis de Sales and Jane, Catherine of Siena and Raymond all began their relationships through spiritual direction. But, because the women in those relationships were spiritually strong and advanced in their own rights, the relationships quickly went from one-sided guidance to mutual spiritual support.

In his book *Light in the Dark Ages: The Friendship of Francis and Clare of Assisi,* Jon M. Sweeney wrote about the way Francis and Clare's relationship developed. It moved from one in which Clare depended upon Francis for guidance to

one where Clare and Francis were offering each other advice and guidance:

> They were two strong, magnetic personalities
> who could communicate with each other eas-
> ily by glance, note, or shared prayer, whether
> they were in the same place at the same time or
> not. They were likely together on fewer than a
> dozen occasions over the space of twenty years,
> most of them only for a matter of hours. But
> they understood each other, supported each
> other, and complemented each other's strengths
> and weaknesses. . . . When Francis cut Clare's
> hair (as a sign of her tonsure, or promise to live
> for Christ) on that fascinating first evening—
> after she had run away from home to join him
> and the friars—there was no scent of perfume
> in the air. Clare was immediately a *brother*.[9]

Spiritual direction can become spiritual friendship
when the two people involved begin to view each other as
spiritual "equals," where advice and direction give way to
spiritual companionship and solidarity. It is, in essence, a
community of two.

Maureen Moran met Chris when she was taking spiritual
direction courses as part of her work for a hospice program
in upstate New York. She got to know Chris and asked her
if she would become her spiritual director. From there, the
relationship grew into a spiritual friendship.

"I have other friends whom I pray with and pray for,
but as a spiritual friend, Chris is the most important," remembered Maureen. "She doesn't really advise me. She
'companions' me. . . . She has really helped encourage me
to make my life more contemplative. I like the way she is

walking with me. It's not a social friendship. We don't go to movies. For me she really is a spiritual companion."

When Maureen was later diagnosed with ovarian cancer, her friendship with Chris took on even deeper significance. Although they had stopped spiritual direction, Maureen's illness prompted her to return to the formal direction Chris had provided in the past.

"I certainly have lots of friends who are spiritual, and we talk about spiritual things, but because Chris and I have known each other for all these years . . . it has become more intimate."

Diamond in the Rough

A community of spiritual friends can consist of two dozen people from an annual retreat or a few people from a scripture study group. No matter the size of our spiritual community, we have a spiritual support group that has the potential to deepen faith connections as well as social connections. No matter how we choose to bond—in prayer, over coffee, through honest conversations, with humor or music, in the midst of a service project—spiritual friendships will grow and deepen. And most of us will be changed from the inside out.

"Independence is a pervasive and popular myth," wrote John Michael Talbot, singer, songwriter, and founder of the Arkansas-based Brothers and Sisters of Charity, in *The Lessons of St. Francis: How to Bring Simplicity and Spirituality into Your Daily Life*. "But the truth is that nothing in our universe is truly independent. Nature is an interdependent network. The cosmos is communication. God wants us to be more interdependent as well, not only for our own good but for the good of the world as well."[10]

Being interdependent means being willing to take risks, to be vulnerable, to open our hearts and bare our souls. And that's not always easy. If the goal is to build a community of spiritual friends, it's important to trust in the process. We need to believe that God's hand is at work in our lives. We have to learn to recognize the diamonds in the rough—those people who may not initially seem to have much in common with us but end up in our lives for reasons we can't explain. When we accept these blessings and begin to seek out ways to nurture the early bonds of spiritual friendship, we will find ourselves with a growing community of people who can see beyond the "mask" we sometimes wear in public, people who know our hearts.

Food for Thought

1. What are the greatest obstacles to your spiritual life? How might a community of spiritual friends provide support?

2. Reflect on the advice St. Benedict offered about life's proper balance: solitude alongside community, work alongside prayer, friends alongside strangers. How can you apply this philosophy to your life? How can you use it to build up your spiritual life and reach out to others?

3. What groups, organizations, events in your life might lend themselves to fostering a community of spiritual

friends? How can you deepen connections with friends
in order to create a community?

Meditation

We are not meant to be solitary figures
walking a lonely path toward heaven.
We are meant for God and for each other.
We are one body with many parts,
sharing our gifts and growing in faith.
Today we pray for the grace
to recognize the friends in our midst,
to open our eyes, our hearts, our minds
to the possibility of what God has planned.
We long for a community of friends
to journey with us, and we know now
that through trust and abandonment,
we will be given exactly what we need.

Chapter 10

Pilgrimage:
Walking Together in the World

To him who is everywhere present and everywhere entire we approach not by our feet but by our hearts.

—St. Augustine

Bishop Howard Hubbard of Albany, New York, remembers the first crisis of his vocation with vivid clarity. He was not yet a priest but a seminarian at North American College in Rome. His father had died, but the seminarian learned that he would not be allowed to return to the United States for his father's funeral.

"That was the greatest crisis I had in terms of my own vocational pursuit," he recalls. "I remember talking to Matthew Clark about what I should do and how I should handle this deprivation. His journey with me during that crisis served to deepen our bond. . . . To have someone like Matthew Clark with you at that time, to walk with you and support you and encourage you, it's something that is deeply embedded on my psyche."

Bishop Hubbard is referring with such fondness to his friendship with Bishop Matthew Clark of Rochester, New York. The two met more than fifty years ago, when they attended minor seminary together in Albany. During those years, these seminarians became close friends as they attended classes, played sports, and served together as counselors at a local summer camp.

"We would talk about our hopes and aspirations for the future and whatever challenges we were facing in the seminary. We developed a close friendship that has lasted the rest of our lives," Bishop Hubbard said, recalling with incredible detail the day-to-day development of their friendship.

The two men have shadowed each other, in many respects, throughout their vocations. Both from the Albany Diocese, they went on to attend seminary at North American College and were ordained in Rome one year apart. After ordination as priests, Matthew Clark returned to Albany to serve in the chancery office, and Fr. Howard Hubbard returned to take up his assignment at the Cathedral of the Immaculate Conception.

"We started taking days off together and then vacations. Since 1965, we have vacationed together in Cape Cod every year. The only year we missed was the year we went to Rome and Sicily," Bishop Hubbard said. When on vacation, the two priests begin each day by concelebrating Mass together. "That's an integral part of our day."

The friendship between these two churchmen has flourished and grown stronger over five decades. It supported them when they returned to Rome to pursue advanced degrees, when they were both named bishops of New York dioceses as relatively young men, and when they regularly confront the challenges of being Church leaders. Bishops Hubbard and Clark have relied on each other for support, honest advice, encouragement, and prayer.

"To have another person who is a soul mate as a sounding board is very helpful. . . . People know that we have a very special bond," Bishop Hubbard explained, joking that people often confuse them even though they look nothing alike. He and Bishop Clark talk every week or two on the phone, more often when one of them is struggling with something. And, he stressed, they like to have fun, whether it's joking with one another or catching a ball game. When Bishop Clark celebrated his thirtieth anniversary as the Bishop of Rochester, the diocese gave him two tickets to a Yankee-Red Sox game. But the diocese also dictated to whom the second ticket had to go—Bishop Howard Hubbard.

For Bishop Hubbard, the real moment of truth in their friendship came in 2004, when he was falsely accused of sexual misconduct. Bishop Hubbard was on vacation in Florida at the time. Bishop Clark had planned to be there but couldn't travel because of pacemaker surgery. When he received the call at 4 p.m. telling him that an accusation had been made, Bishop Hubbard rushed to the airport, giving instructions for five people to be called immediately: the papal nuncio, the cardinal of New York, Bishop Hubbard's two sisters, and Bishop Clark.

"I called Bishop Clark from the airport. He knew how devastated I was. The following morning when I got to the office for the press conference, he was there. It meant the world to me that he would come and stand by me in that hour of need," he remembered.

Bishop Hubbard said that, in addition to sharing their own lived experience of the priesthood and of being diocesan bishops, he and Bishop Clark share "our understanding of Church, our relationship with Christ, what sustains us during times of adversity, what energizes us, challenges us, discourages us, disillusions us, and put that into the context of discipleship."

"On an in-depth level, our friendship has certainly deepened my own spiritual life, and I have certainly taken inspiration from the way Bishop Clark has handled the challenges of episcopal ministry and the challenges of his health," Bishop Hubbard said. He noted that Bishop Clark has faced many physical ailments as "part and parcel of uniting his suffering to the suffering of Christ."

"He did it in the context of a pilgrim on a journey of faith," Bishop Hubbard said, with obvious admiration and brotherly love.

Approaching Life with a Pilgrim Heart

Illness can be a pilgrimage. Marriage can be a pilgrimage. Any moment, really, where we recognize God's presence can be a pilgrimage. Pilgrimage doesn't mean reaching a particular geographical location. Instead, it refers to reaching a deep interior place. Life itself is a pilgrimage, whether we crisscross the continents visiting great shrines and sacred places or never even cross a state line. We are all on a journey toward God. It is up to us to decide whether that journey will be about simply surviving the daily challenges or becoming a pilgrim on the road to union with our Creator.

Spiritual friends are natural companions on the pilgrim journey. Even when they can't be physically present to us for some reason, they can be present to us spiritually through shared prayers, conversations, discussions about spiritual readings, and simply talking about their lives.

In their book *The Journey: A Guide for the Modern Pilgrim*, authors Maria Ruiz Scaperlanda and Michael Scaperlanda talk about both the literal and figurative pilgrimages we experience, pointing out that a pilgrimage "increases our capacity to love."

"In fact, pilgrimage gives us ample opportunity to love and to be loved. Although pilgrimage is often lonely travel, it is never unaccompanied. Whether we see them or not, or know them or not, others journey with us," Maria wrote.[1]

Michael Scaperlanda walked the Camino de Santiago Compostela, the Way of St. James, in 2009. The famous pilgrimage route winds some twelve hundred miles through Europe, ending in Compostela in northern Spain where the remains of the apostle St. James the Great are said to be buried. When Michael first planned the pilgrimage, two friends were going to join him. In the end, they were unable to make it, but he carried on alone. They were "prayer partners in the journey," he said, explaining that he didn't always feel the need to be so connected to friends and family. Maria, who had already walked the Camino, has taught him about the importance of sharing his life with friends and family—whether face-to-face, in prayer, or by phone, Facebook, or e-mail.

"Since we are incarnate creatures, spiritual friendship requires incarnate friendship . . . and the incarnation is best seen—at least Jesus suggested this—in the small seemingly insignificant moments of life," Michael wrote in an e-mail to me just before he left on his pilgrimage. "I used to think it

was in the grand moments, the great events of happiness or
sorrow, where I could come together with another person,
but I now think the little moments are where the real action
is. When your spiritual friends know you at this level, they
get a better feel for the rhythm of your life, and they have
a better ability to pray for your needs, ask you the questions that need asking, and make the observations that need
observing."

Michael told me that he saw that reality come into play
when he felt scattered, distracted, and easily annoyed by
others. He shared his feelings with his wife and spiritual
friend, Maria. "She asked me whether I just wanted a listening ear or whether she could make an observation. I gave
her permission, and she reminded me that the moment I
committed to the Camino, that pilgrimage had started and
that the tempter would work to make the pilgrimage less
successful," Michael recalled. "That to me is an example of
the relational back and forth of spiritual friendship. She saw
something in my sharing that I didn't see. She didn't impose
her observation but asked, and I immediately saw what she
was talking about."

Maria has made many pilgrimages around the world.
She is quick to stress that the pilgrim journey is a metaphor
for our lives. Even if we do not set foot on a path toward a
popular and sacred destination, we continue on our own
pilgrimages.

"The big moments that become pilgrimages in our family's lives—illness, a project, a child's problem, a marriage
challenge—and the actual pilgrimages that we take are all
meant to be guide posts, beacons of light to point out the

way for the majority of our lives," Maria told me when I asked about her experience of pilgrimage and the spiritual friendship she shares with her husband. "The mundane, everyday, seemingly unimportant moments of being a family—they are all meant to remind me of God's presence in the thick and thin of it all. In making lunches and cleaning dishes, in making huge decisions about our children's education and our jobs, and in the midst of a crisis that is so dark that I can't see my own feet to know where I'm walking, it's all about what I believe. Either God is NOW here—or God is nowhere. The letters are the same, but you get the idea."

Maria told me that writing their book was also a pilgrimage for her and for Michael. Friends and fellow writers warned them that writing a book together might stress their relationship, and both approached the project with a little anxiety. Maria and Michael wrote separately of their own pilgrimage experiences. Then they shared their writings with each other and saw a greater power at work.

"What happened was amazing. Maybe it's because we had so many people worried about us that their prayers were extra diligent on our behalf, but in all honesty, reading each other's writing was a delight. We even found that the Holy Spirit had directed each of us—working separately, mind you—to some of the same stories in our marriage, even some of the most difficult moments in our marriage. We didn't plan on talking about it, it came out as we wrote. And then we found out that this happened to each of us without talking about it. I don't believe in coincidences, and this is why: God was clearly in charge of that project and directed our minds and hearts to what he wanted told in the writing."

In their book, Maria wrote about the conscious decision to approach life either as tourist or pilgrim. What she meant was that only when we recognize God's presence in our lives can we begin the interior and essential pilgrimage. When we walk this path, aided by spiritual friends who can listen, observe, pray, and advise us, we get closer and closer to our true selves and our ultimate destination.

"This is what the spiritual friendship of marriage is all about for me—trusting that God is at work in my life, in my husband's life, and therefore in our marriage," Maria told me. "Sometimes I can't see it. Often I am afraid and full of anxiety about it. But that doesn't mean that God is not there. Whether I recognize him in the quotidian aspects of my life or not, it doesn't change the fact that God is present."

Learning to Be a Pilgrim

It's easy to romanticize the idea of pilgrimage and miss the real meaning of this important aspect of our spiritual lives and spiritual friendships. We can get caught up in the image of a pilgrim as world traveler. We may think we must traverse the narrow streets of a foreign city to find God. In reality, our pilgrim journey is about traversing a much more difficult path, a path to an interior destination where God resides in our hearts.

In an article titled "The Way of the Pilgrim," Dominican Father Michael Fones, co-director of the Catherine of Siena Institute in Colorado, explained that everyday pilgrimages often lead us to places just as deep and meaningful as more far-flung journeys.

"A few weeks ago I had the opportunity to take a few day hikes in the Rocky Mountains west of Denver with another Dominican friend of mine. A simple walk can have the effect of a pilgrimage if it is undertaken with a conscious abandonment of our daily cares so that we can focus our senses on the world around us: the warmth of the sun or the patter of rain, the shudder of leaves on a soft breeze, the aroma of pine or eucalyptus. In these moments I find it easy to reflect on the loveliness and unfathomed creativity of God," Father Fones wrote.[2]

I recently had an opportunity to experience an "everyday pilgrimage" when I went on a silent, contemplative retreat at a rustic lodge. The lodge was set back from a pristine lake in New York's Adirondack Mountains. It was not a pilgrimage in the traditional sense since I didn't travel to a specific sacred site where saints had walked before me. However, it was a pilgrimage in the sense that it transported me to a place deep within myself. Surrounded by the wonder of God's creation, I burrowed down into my cluttered and chaotic interior life to sweep out some space and make room for God. I may not have been walking the roads of Assisi, but I was walking an equally foreign road of single-minded devotion and discovery.

Not long after my silent retreat, I made a weekend pilgrimage with my son, Noah, to the National Shrine of the North American Martyrs in Auriesville, New York. There, I was able to walk the grounds where saints were martyred and where Blessed Kateri Tekakwitha was born. It was a pilgrimage in the more traditional sense, and I felt a deep peace in this place so steeped in faith. At night, as I slept in a tent on the grounds, and by day, as I walked the paths with other pilgrims, I could feel the power of the pilgrim journey. Perhaps for the first time, my pilgrim heart was awakened, and I realized that we are all pilgrims.

Tracing Our Pilgrim Roots

In his book *Lourdes Diary: Seven Days at the Grotto of Massabielle*, Father James Martin, S.J., wrote that pilgrimage is part of our tradition, dating back to the beginning of Christianity.

"The disciples were, in so many ways, pilgrims. And, of course, Jesus himself would die in Jerusalem during a time of pilgrimage," Father Martin wrote, explaining that in the centuries that followed, the importance of pilgrimage took hold in the growing Church. The first Christians often visited the tombs of the martyrs. By the Middle Ages, pilgrims traveled to pray in the Holy Land where Jesus lived and died. Modern pilgrims still visit Jerusalem and Rome, Marian shrines around the world, and countless other sacred sites.[3]

Pilgrimage is not, of course, a strictly Christian practice. It predates Christianity. Believers from all religious backgrounds journey to visit holy places and express their faith through their physical presence. It is, at once, an act of devotion, an act of thanksgiving, and an act of penance. From the ancient Egyptians, Greeks, and Aztecs to modern-day Hindus, Buddhists, and Muslims, pilgrimage is an important and sometimes required devotional practice. A pilgrimage is not a tour or a getaway but a journey focused on faith.

"Pilgrimages are a time-honored way of fostering reliance on God, so dependent are pilgrims on the grace of God, which manifests itself in the charity and kindness of fellow pilgrims and in those we meet along the way. The time of travel is also what one of my spiritual directors called a liminal time—a transitional moment, or an in-between space. We find ourselves caught between one place and another, and during these times we can be especially aware of God. Removed from our comfortable routines, we are naturally more aware of our fundamental reliance on God, and are therefore more often more open to grace," explained Father Martin.[4] He traveled to Lourdes for the first time as a chaplain to the Order of Malta, a worldwide charitable Catholic organization. He brought along two of his Jesuit friends.

"We need not travel to southern France to encounter God's presence in our lives," he explained. "God dwells within us already, and just as important as the grotto of Lourdes, where Mary spoke to Bernadette in 1858, is the grotto of our hearts, where God speaks to us every day."[5]

Walking Together

Perhaps, like Father Martin, you will be lucky enough to make a traditional pilgrimage with a spiritual friend or a group of friends through a parish or organized tour. If you can't make an overseas pilgrimage, maybe you can find something closer to home. It could be a local shrine, an historic cathedral, a church where a saint was baptized. If you can go on a pilgrimage with others, whether it's around the corner or across the globe, by all means, do it.

Don't worry if you simply can't go on a traditional pilgrimage with a spiritual friend. There are lots of options, more options than you may imagine. Spiritual friendships do not require constant face-to-face visits or trips. Instead, they require endless heart-to-heart conversations and shared prayers, something you can do no matter where you live or how much time and money you have for travel.

The obvious place to start here is with prayer. If you are looking for only one thing that will connect you to your spiritual friends, it should be prayer. Although private prayer is essential to our spiritual lives, we need to join our prayers to the prayers of our friends. Yes, we can pray *for* our friends and their intentions, but it's even more powerful to pray *with* our friends, even if we are physically separated.

Talk to your spiritual friend or group of friends to identify a prayer time that suits everyone's schedule. This will be a time when you are all praying together even when you are apart. It could be first thing in the morning or at noon or at 3 p.m. or just before bed. If you can't pray at the same time, perhaps you can say the same prayers. You may decide to pray the Liturgy of the Hours or the Rosary. Or, if you don't have a lot of time, you might agree to say just an Our Father, a Hail Mary, a Glory Be.

This type of joint prayer also allows for reflections and prayers based on the liturgical seasons. During Advent, you can pray for each other when you light the Advent wreath before evening meals. During Lent, you can offer particular sacrifices for a friend's intentions. One year, my friend

Bill and I decided that all through Holy Week, we would pray at a certain time but would not talk to or e-mail each other. Our connection would be strictly through prayer. So every day at 1 p.m., Bill and I would pray and remember the other. Something about the arrangement echoed the starkness of Holy Week, making the experience that much more powerful.

Margaret Robertson and her friend Brenda allowed prayer to cement and strengthen their friendship. When Margaret traveled to the National Basilica of the Immaculate Conception in Washington, DC, and to other churches and monasteries in the region, she brought the prayer intentions of Brenda and Brenda's family with her. Likewise, while Brenda was traveling through Ireland, she was remembering Margaret in prayer.

Margaret, Brenda, and their friends, Mary Rita and Cheryl, also have another more unusual prayer connection. Whenever any of them spots a digital clock with the same numbers across—for example, 2:22 or 4:44—they stop what they are doing and say a prayer for each other whether they are together or apart. It is a spontaneous but spiritual connection.

Whether spiritual friends are bishops celebrating Mass together on vacation or laywomen attending nocturnal adoration together at a parish church, they can continually deepen their faith connections through many different devotions and practices. An endless variety of devotions and styles of prayer make it easy for spiritual friends to explore many holy paths together. No need to sign up for a pilgrimage tour.

In "The Way of the Pilgrim," an article on the Catherine of Siena Institute website, Father Fones wrote that prayer is at the heart of any pilgrimage when the desired outcome is atonement, healing, or a deepening relationship with God. "In fact, one might propose that prayer itself is a pilgrimage, whether it be in the form of a lengthy retreat, an hour before the Blessed Sacrament, or a response to the Lord's invitation to a few moments of stillness in the midst of a busy day," he wrote.[6]

Prayer is not the only option. Another way to connect with a spiritual friend is through shared spiritual reading. Choose a spiritual book that you are both interested in reading. Talk or e-mail about what you're feeling as you read. Jot down questions you have or points you want to discuss. Share passages that you find particularly moving.

You can take the above suggestion even further and write in a spiritual journal each day. Then, if you are comfortable with the idea, swap journals so you can enter more deeply into the spiritual journey of the other. This is an especially good idea if one of you can go on a traditional pilgrimage but the other cannot. If you are traveling to a sacred place, write down your thoughts and what you are experiencing. Later, share the journal with your friend when you return home. The pilgrimage journal will not only allow your spiritual friend to "accompany" you on that pilgrimage. It will also leave you with a lasting record of what you were thinking and feeling when you made the journey yourself. You can go back to revisit the place again and again through your own journal.

Music can be a powerful connection that often gets over-looked. When I went on my Cornerstone women's retreat, the retreat team gave each of us a CD with all the music used during the program. When I am working around the house or driving around town, I put on the music and am suddenly transported back to the retreat center. I can visualize the moment when we were all standing around a table taking turns stirring and kneading the dough for the Communion bread. I remember the many hours we spent sharing our faith stories through tears and laughter.

Don't be afraid to use technology to your advantage. Clearly, technology can isolate us, but when used for good, even our high-tech gadgets can be agents of transformation. Send your spiritual friend an e-mail with a quote from your favorite saint, or text-message your friend on a birthday or anniversary, promising extra prayers. Or share spiritual websites or blogs that you find particularly helpful. There are so many ways to stay connected through the days and weeks until you can have that heart-to-heart talk or that personal visit or even that long-planned pilgrimage.

Make Your Own Rules

In the seventeenth century, during the days of St. Francis de Sales and St. Jane de Chantal, the only way to stay connected was to visit or to write letters. As we know, even letters could take weeks to arrive. Although technology can work against friendship if we are not careful, it can be a blessing when approached from the right perspective and with the right intention.

I've often heard people say that if St. Paul were alive to-day, he'd be blogging and texting. He would use any means he could to spread the Good News. In other words, we can truly use technology as an evangelization tool, finding ways to make it work for us and for the building up of the King-dom here on earth.

I was recently looking at my e-mail inbox. It tends to get rather cluttered with messages I don't want to delete. There, amid the countless e-mails related to work, volunteer proj-ects, or school homework assignments for my children, were spiritual e-mails from spiritual friends. Those are things that I hold onto so that I can go back and re-read them when I'm in need of a spiritual lift. It was a reminder to me that I have been blessed in abundance with spiritual friends from all walks of life. These friends are fellow pilgrims.

With the right touch, our high-tech, high-speed style of communication can be the answer to a prayer. It can give us constant and immediate connection to the soul friends who walk with us on this journey toward heaven, this pilgrim-age to the only place that matters: the heart of God.

Food for Thought

1. What is your vision of pilgrimage? Even if you cannot physically go on pilgrimage, can you think of ways that you can journey toward God in your mind and heart?

2. Consider setting up a prayer "schedule" with a spiritual friend so that you can stay connected even when you can't visit or talk. What types of prayers,

devotions, and spiritual readings would work well in
this prayer partnership?

3. Pilgrimage is a journey of the heart. You could view
your entire life as a pilgrimage. What do you need for
this journey—materially, emotionally, spiritually? Who
are the companions you would like to accompany you
on this interior walk?

Meditation

So often this journey through life
can feel like a daily struggle,
a race to accomplish more,
buy more, be more.
Today we pray for the wisdom
to take a step back and look
at the bigger picture.
The true meaning of our journey
is not about earthly things but about
matters of the heart
and longings of the spirit.
We open our arms to those companions
who join us on this pilgrimage of love.
We recognize that we are not meant
to walk this road one by one,
but side by side.

Notes

Chapter 1: Companionship
1. Merton, *Zen and the Birds of Appetite*, 60–61.
2. Merton, *Passion for Peace*, 260–262.
3. Aelred of Rievaulx, *Spiritual Friendship*, 35.
4. Ibid., 40.
5. Ibid., 41.

Chapter 2: Acceptance
1. Francis de Sales, *Treatise on the Love of God*, 161.
2. Ibid., 55.
3. Wilson, *Homecoming*, 174.
4. Ibid., 218.

Chapter 3: Love of God
1. Francis de Sales, *Introduction to the Devout Life*, 131.
2. Ibid., 131.
3. Nouwen in Francis de Sales, *Francis de Sales, Jane de Chantal*, 4.
4. Francis de Sales, *Francis de Sales, Jane de Chantal*, 4.
5. Ibid., 68.
6. Lewis, *Four Loves*, 65.
7. Ibid., 58.
8. Ibid., 57.
9. Duriez, *Tolkien and C. S. Lewis*, 176–177.
10. Lewis, *Four Loves*, 72.
11. Ibid., 66.
12. Francis de Sales, *Introduction to the Devout Life*, 131.
13. Ibid., 131.

Chapter 4: Humility, Honesty, and Charity
1. Francis de Sales, *Francis de Sales, Jane de Chantal*, 149.
2. Francis de Sales, *Introduction to the Devout Life*, 96.
3. Ibid., 127.
4. Ibid., 128.
5. Talbot, *Lessons of St. Francis*, 116.
6. Sweeney, *Friendship of Francis and Clare of Assisi*, 17.
7. Francis et al., *Francis and Clare*, 103.
8. Straub, *The Sun and Moon Over Assisi*, 345.

Chapter 5: Communication
1. Nouwen, *Life of the Beloved*, 30.
2. Wild, *Compassionate Fire*, 13.
3. Ibid., 76.
4. Francis de Sales, *Introduction to the Devout Life*, 127.
5. Ibid.
6. Ibid., 137.
7. Nouwen in Francis de Sales, *Francis de Sales, Jane de Chantal*, 5.
8. Ibid., 5.
9. Francis de Sales, *Francis de Sales, Jane de Chantal*, 147.
10. Wild, *Compassionate Fire*, 33.
11. Ibid., 41.
12. Pope Benedict XVI, *New Technologies, New Relationships.*
13. Ibid.

Chapter 6: Kindred Spirits
1. Paul, *Friendship Crisis*, 74–75.
2. Pope St. Gregory, *Dialogues*, 102–103.
3. Ibid., 103.
4. Thérèse of Lisieux, *Story of a Soul*, 39.
5. Ibid., 42.
6. Pope Benedict XVI, *Conferral of the Honorary Citizenship*, August 21, 1988.
7. Ibid.
8. Francis de Sales, *Introduction to the Devout Life*, 128.
9. Popcak, *For Better . . . Forever!*, 219.
10. Ibid., 223.
11. Ibid., 220.
12. Ibid., 222.
13. Katz, *Running to the Mountain*, 31.
14. Dziwisz, *Life with Karol*, 8.
15. Ibid., 4.
16. Ibid., 259.
17. Ibid., 260.
18. Ibid., 3.

Chapter 7: Celibate Love
1. Schnackenburgh, *Friend We Have in Jesus*, 33.
2. Rolheiser, *Forgotten Among the Lilies*, 36.
3. Ibid., 37–38.
4. Norris, *Cloister Walk*, 122.

5. Ibid., 123.
6. Vann, *To Heaven with Diana*, 88.
7. Ibid., 88.
8. Ibid., 90.
9. O'Malley, *Saintly Companions*, 155.
10. Norris, *Cloister Walk*, 122.

Chapter 8: Commitment
1. Scott, *Catholic Passion*, 216.
2. Nouwen, *Life of the Beloved*, 117.
3. Ibid.
4. Pope Benedict XVI, *Spe Salvi*, 15–16.
5. Francis de Sales, *Introduction to the Devout Life*, 131.
6. Aelred of Rievaulx, *Spiritual Friendship*, 107.
7. White, *Charlotte's Web*, 164.

Chapter 9: Community
1. Taylor, *Spirituality for Everyday Living*, 53.
2. Lewis, *Four Loves*, 89.
3. Ellsberg, ed., *Dorothy Day: Selected Writings*, xxiii.
4. Ibid, xxvi.
5. Ibid.
6. Ibid., 44.
7. Ibid., 46.
8. Coy, ed., *Revolution of the Heart*, 24.
9. Sweeney, *Light in the Dark Ages*, 22.
10. Talbot, *Lessons of St. Francis*, 145.

Chapter 10: Pilgrimage
1. Scaperlanda and Scaperlanda, *Journey*, 91.
2. Fones, "The Way of the Pilgrim."
3. Martin, *Lourdes Diary*, 31.
4. Ibid., 32.
5. Ibid., 65.
6. Fones, "The Way of the Pilgrim."

Bibliography

Aelred of Rievaulx. *Spiritual Friendship*. Notre Dame: Ave Maria Press, 2008.

Coy, Patrick G., ed. *Revolution of the Heart: Essays on the Catholic Worker*. Philadelphia: Temple University Press, 1988.

Duriez, Colin. *Tolkien and C. S. Lewis: The Gift of Friendship*. New York: Paulist Press, 2003.

Dziwisz, Cardinal Stanislaw. *A Life with Karol: My Forty-Year Friendship with the Man Who Became Pope*. New York: Doubleday, 2008.

Ellsberg, Robert, ed. *Dorothy Day: Selected Writings*. New York: Orbis Books, 2005.

Fones, Michael. "The Way of the Pilgrim." Catherine of Siena Institute, www.siena.org/library/EScribe/07Sep.htm.

Francis of Assisi, Regis J. Armstrong, Ignatius C. Brady, and Clare of Assisi. *Francis and Clare: The Complete Works*. New York: Paulist Press, 1982.

Francis de Sales. *Francis de Sales, Jane de Chantal: Letters of Spiritual Direction*. New York: Paulist Press, 1988.

―――. *Introduction to the Devout Life*. New York: Gardners Books, 2007.

―――. *Treatise on the Love of God*. Charlotte, NC: Tan Books and Publishers, 1975.

Katz, Jon. *Running to the Mountain: A Journey of Faith and Change*. New York: Villard, 1999.

Lewis, C. S. *The Four Loves*. New York: Harcourt, 1960.

Martin, James. *Lourdes Diary: Seven Days at the Grotto of Massabielle*. Chicago: Loyola Press, 2006.

Merton, Thomas. *Passion for Peace: The Social Essays*. New York: Crossroad, 1995.

―――. *Zen and the Birds of Appetite*. New York: New Directions, 1968.

Norris, Kathleen. *The Cloister Walk*. New York: Riverhead Books, 1996.

Nouwen, Henri J. M. *Life of the Beloved: Spiritual Living in a Secular World*. New York: Crossroad, 1992.

O'Malley, Vincent J. *Saintly Companions: A Cross-Reference of Sainted Relationships*. New York: Alba House, 1995.

Paul, Marla. *The Friendship Crisis: Finding, Making, and Keeping Friends When You're Not a Kid Anymore*. Emmaus, PA: Rodale, 2004.

Popcak, Gregory K. *For Better . . . Forever!: A Catholic Guide to Lifelong Marriage*. Huntington, IN: Our Sunday Visitor Publishing, 1999.

Pope Benedict XVI. *Conferral of the Honorary Citizenship*. August 21, 1988.

———. *New Technologies, New Relationships*. Message for the 43rd World Day of Communications, 2009.

———. *On Christian Hope: Spe Salvi, Encyclical Letter*. Washington, DC: United States Conference of Catholic Bishops, 2007.

Pope St. Gregory. *Saint Gregory the Great: Dialogues*. New York: Fathers of the Church, 1959.

Putnam, Robert D. *Bowling Alone: The Collapse and Revival of American Community*. New York: Simon & Schuster, 2000.

Rolheiser, Ronald. *Forgotten Among the Lilies: Learning to Love Beyond Our Fears*. Cincinnati : St. Anthony Messenger Press, 2007.

Scaperlanda, Maria Ruiz and Michael Scaperlanda. *The Journey: A Guide for the Modern Pilgrim*. Chicago: Loyola Press, 2004.

Schnackenburgh, Rudolf. *The Friend We Have in Jesus*. Louisville, KY: Westminster John Knox Press, 1997.

Scott, David. *The Catholic Passion: Rediscovering the Power and Beauty of the Faith*. Chicago: Loyola Press, 2005.

Straub, Gerard Thomas. *The Sun and Moon Over Assisi: A Personal Encounter with Francis and Clare*. Cincinnati: St. Anthony Messenger Press, 2000.

Sweeney, Jon M. *Light in the Dark Ages: The Friendship of Francis and Clare of Assisi*. Brewster, MA: Paraclete Press, 2007.

Talbot, John Michael. *The Lessons of St. Francis*. New York: Plume, 1998.

Taylor, Brian C. *Spirituality for Everyday Living: An Adaptation of the Rule of St. Benedict*. Collegeville, MN: Liturgical Press, 1989.

Vann, Gerald. *To Heaven with Diana!: A Study of Jordan of Saxony and Diana d'Andalo*. New York: iUniverse, 2006.

White, E. B. *Charlotte's Web*. New York: Harper Collins, 1952.

Wild, Robert A., ed. *Compassionate Fire: The Letters of Thomas Merton and Catherine de Hueck Doherty*. Notre Dame: Ave Maria Press, 2009.

Wilson, Julie R. *Homecoming: A Prophetic Study of Ruth*. Grand Haven, MI: FaithWalk, 2002.

Mary DeTurris Poust is an author, columnist, journalist, and blogger who has written for dozens of Catholic and secular publications over the last twenty-five years. She is the author of *The Complete Idiot's Guide to the Catholic Catechism* and *Parenting a Grieving Child*. Poust was a senior correspondent and contributing editor for *Our Sunday Visitor* newspaper for fourteen years and is currently a daily contributor to *Our Sunday Visitor's* popular blog, "OSV Daily Take." Her award-winning monthly column "Life Lines" has been published in *Catholic New York* since 2001. She also writes about family, faith, and the spiritual journey at her own blog, "Not Strictly Spiritual." She has worked for the dioceses of Metuchen, New Jersey, and Austin, Texas, as well as the Archdiocese of New York, where she served as managing editor of *Catholic New York*. She lives in upstate New York with her husband and three children. Visit Mary online at www.marydeturrispoust.com.